Samuel Beckett and
Bram van Velde

Conversations with Samuel Beckett and Bram van Velde

Charles Juliet

translated by Tracy Cooke, Aude Jeanson,
Axel Nesme, Morgaine Reinl, and Janey Tucker

Dalkey Archive Press
Champaign and London

Originally published in French by Editions Fata Morgana, Montpellier,
as *Rencontres avec Bram van Velde*, 1973 (expanded edition, 1978);
and *Rencontres avec Samuel Beckett*, 1986
Rencontres avec Bram van Velde copyright © P.O.L. éditeur, 1998
Rencontres avec Samuel Beckett copyright © P.O.L. éditeur, 1999
Conversations with Bram van Velde translation copyright © Janey Tucker, 1995;
Morgaine Reinl, Aude Jeanson, 2009
Conversations with Samuel Beckett translation copyright © Tracy Cooke,
Axel Nesme, 2009
Notes copyright © Adriaan van der Weel and Ruud Hisgen, 1995
First Dalkey Archive edition, 2009

Library of Congress Cataloging-in-Publication Data

Juliet, Charles, 1934-
 [Rencontres avec Samuel Beckett. English.]
 Conversations with Samuel Beckett, and Bram van Velde / by Charles
Juliet ; translated by Tracy Cooke, Axel Nesme, Janey Tucker, Morgaine
Reinl, and Aude Jeanson. -- 1st Dalkey Archive ed.
  p. cm.
 Originally published in French as Rencontres avec Samuel Beckett,
and Rencontres avec Bram van Velde.
 ISBN 978-1-56478-531-2 (pbk. : alk. paper)
 1. Beckett, Samuel, 1906-1989--Interviews. 2. Authors, French--20th
century--Interviews. 3. Authors, Irish--20th century--Interviews. 4.
Velde, Bram van, 1895-1981--Interviews. 5.
Painters--Netherlands--Interviews. I. Cooke, Tracy. II. Nesme, Axel.
III. Juliet, Charles, 1934- Rencontres avec Bram van Velde. English.
IV. Title.
 PQ2603.E378Z47413 2009
 848'.91409--dc22
                              2009026227

Partially funded by a grant from the Illinois Arts Council, a state agency, and by the
University of Illinois at Urbana-Champaign

www.dalkeyarchive.com

Cover: design and composition by Danielle Dutton; illustration by Nicholas Motte
Printed on permanent/durable acid-free paper and bound in the United States of America

Contents

Conversations with
Samuel Beckett

translated by Tracy Cooke and Axel Nesme

*Where we have, at one and the same time,
darkness and light, we also have the inexplicable.*

Samuel Beckett

I buzz the intercom to his apartment. He tells me to come up. As I step out of the elevator, I almost bump into him. He has been waiting for me in the hallway. We enter his study. I sit down on a small sofa opposite his desk, while he takes his place on a stool at a slight angle to me. He is already in the usual posture he assumes whenever he is sitting unoccupied: one leg wrapped around the other, his chin resting on his hand, shoulders hunched, eyes fixed on the floor.

Silence sets in, and I know it will not be easy to break it. Strange, I think to myself, to ask questions of a man who is himself a question. His gaze is evasive, but when I sense that his eyes are trying to seek mine, it is I who look away. Here I am, in the presence of this man whose work has given me so much, and with whom, in my solitude, I have held endless dialogues, so that for me he is already like a friend, yet I realize that for him I am only a stranger. Throughout our discussion I will have difficulty reconciling such violently opposed realities.

The silence is such that it seems solid. I suddenly remember with some apprehension that Beckett is quite capable of meeting with someone—Maurice Nadeau[1] told me this—and then leaving one or two hours later without ever having said a single word.

I observe him discreetly. He is grave, somber. His brow is knitted. His gaze unbearably intense. I feel myself beginning to panic, so I force myself—if not to speak—at least to produce a sound.

And in a barely audible voice I begin to explain to him how at the age of twenty-two I tried to read *Molloy*. How I did not understand it, had no idea of its importance. How, for some curious reason, not even intending to read them, I acquired all the works he published afterward. How in the spring of 1965, and completely by chance, I skimmed through a few lines from *Texts for Nothing*. How I could not put the book down and devoured it passionately. How I then became immersed in his work and how it transformed me. How I read each of his works over and over again. How what impressed me most was the odd silence that reigns in *Texts for Nothing*, a silence that can only be reached in the most extreme solitude, when one's being has left everything, forgotten everything, and simply listens to the voice that murmurs when all else has fallen silent. An odd silence, yes, prolonged by the nakedness of speech. Speech without rhetoric, without literature, speech never once drowned out by the bare minimum of fiction required to give shape to what it must articulate.

"Yes," he admits in a hollow voice. "Listening to yourself, it is not literature that you hear."

I know that over the last few months he has been seriously ill. Indeed, this is the reason why our initial meeting, originally scheduled for May 3rd, could not take place. The day before, he had gone to the opening of the Hayden[2] exhibition, and become ill later that night. Mrs. Beckett had greeted me at the door, saying that he had the flu, and we agreed that the scheduled meeting was not cancelled, that it would simply be postponed for a few days. But I waited in vain for a phone call.

Four months later, I found out that he had had an abscess in his lung, and I immediately wondered if this was a long-delayed consequence of that day before the war when, one evening, in the street, with no apparent reason, a tramp had stabbed him.

So I ask him about his health. He answers me. Then the conversation drifts towards old age.

"I have always wanted to be alert and active in my later years—always burning inside, though your body is failing—I have often thought of Yeats. He wrote his best poems after the age of sixty."

In answer to my questions, he tells me about the extremely dark years he lived through after resigning from Trinity College in Dublin. He lived in London first, then in Paris. He gave up a very promising university career, but not because he was thinking of becoming a writer. He lived in a small hotel room near Montparnasse; he felt lost, crushed, without will. He would rise at noon; he barely had enough strength to make it to the nearest café for breakfast. He could do nothing, not even read.

"I had let myself become an Oblomov—" Then he whispers wearily: "There was my wife—it was difficult—"

I ask him other questions, but he can't remember. Or he does not want to recall that period of his life. He speaks of a tunnel, mental twilight . . . Then he says:

"I have always felt as if, inside me, someone had been murdered. Murdered before my birth. I had to find this murdered being. Try to give him life . . . Once I attended a lecture by Jung—he spoke of one of his patients, a young girl . . . Afterwards, as people were leaving, Jung remained silent. And then, as if speaking to himself, and surprised by the discovery he had made, he added: 'In fact, she had never been born.' I have always had the feeling that I too had never been born."

Actually the end of this lecture became an episode in *All That Fall*:

> MRS. ROONEY: I remember once attending a lecture by one of these new mind doctors. I forget what you call them. He spoke—
> MR. ROONEY: A lunatic specialist?
> MRS. ROONEY: No no, just the troubled mind. I was hoping he might shed a little light on my lifelong preoccupation with horses' buttocks.
> MR. ROONEY: A neurologist.
> MRS. ROONEY: No no, just mental distress, the name will come back to me in the night. I remember his telling us the story of a little girl, very strange and unhappy in her ways, and how he treated her unsuccessfully over a period of years and was finally obliged to give up the case. He could find nothing wrong with her, he said. The only thing wrong with her as far as he could see was that she was dying. And she did in fact die, shortly after he washed his hands of her.
> MR. ROONEY: Well? What is there so wonderful about that?
> MRS. ROONEY: No, it was just something he said, and the way he said it, that have haunted me ever since.
> MR. ROONEY: You lie awake at night, tossing to and fro and brooding on it.
> MRS. ROONEY: On it and other . . . wretchedness. (*Pause.*) When he had done with the little girl he stood there motionless for some time, quite two minutes I

should say, looking down at his table. Then he suddenly raised his head and exclaimed, as if he had had a revelation, The trouble with her was she had never been really born! (*Pause.*) He spoke throughout without notes. (*Pause.*) I left before the end.

In 1945 he returned to Ireland to visit his mother, whom he had not seen since the beginning of the war. Then he went back again to see her in 1946, and it was during this visit that he had the brusque revelation of what he had to do.

"I understood things could not go on as they were."

He then tells me about that night in Dublin, at the end of a jetty, while a storm was raging. What he told me is found in this passage from *Krapp's Last Tape*:

> Spiritually a year of profound gloom and indigence until that memorable night in March, at the end of the jetty, in the howling wind, never to be forgotten, when suddenly I saw the whole thing. The vision at last [. . .] What I suddenly saw then was this, that the belief I had been going on all my life, namely (*Krapp switches off impatiently, winds tape forward, switches on again*)—great granite rocks the foam flying up in the light of the light house and the wind-gauge spinning like a propeller, clear to me at last that the dark I have always struggled to keep under is in reality my most (*Krapp curses, switches off, winds tape forward, switches on again*)—unshatterable association until my dissolution of storm and night with the light of the understanding and the fire [. . .]

"I had to reject all the poisons . . ." (By this he probably means intellectual decency, knowledge, the certainties one invents for oneself, the need to dominate life . . .) "I had to find the right language. When I wrote the first sentence of *Molloy*, I didn't know where I was going. And when I completed the first part, I had no idea how I would continue it. It all came like that. Without a single correction. I had planned nothing—worked out nothing ahead of time."

He gets up and takes a rather thick notebook with a faded cover out of a drawer and hands it to me. It is the manuscript of *Waiting for Godot*. The paper in the notebook is of poor quality, dating from the war. The pages are gray, rough. Only the right-hand pages are covered—with very small, slanted writing, almost illegible. I leaf through it, quite moved. Toward the end, the left-hand pages are used, but to read these I need to turn the notebook upside down. It is true: there are no signs of rewriting. As I try to decipher several lines, he whispers:

"It all happened between my hand and the page."

No, he has not read Eastern philosophers.

"They suggest a way out, whereas I felt there was none. One solution—death."

I ask him if he is writing, if he can still write:

"My previous work forbids my pursuing the same kind of work. Of course, I could write more texts like the ones in *Têtes-mortes* (Death's-heads). But I don't want to. I just threw out a short play. Each time, there has to be a step forward."

Long silence.

"Writing has led me to silence."

Long silence.

"Yet I must go on . . . I am up against a wall, but I have to move forward. It's impossible, isn't it? Yet you can still move forward, gain a few miserable millimeters . . ."

But the doctor has given him strict orders. It is time for him to take some medication now, and he apologizes for having to interrupt our talk for a moment.

In the letter I wrote asking to meet with him, I had mentioned that I knew Bram van Velde.

They are old friends, but Bram van Velde lives in Geneva and never writes, so now they have very little contact.

He asks about him.

One of Bram van Velde's paintings is opposite his desk, behind where I am sitting, and I stand up to take a look at it.

It is an enigmatic piece, painted before World War II, during a period of transition.

I know how much Beckett likes this painting, but I am tempted to think that he also acquired it because he wanted to help a painter who was nearly destitute.

While I am still standing, I glance out the window, and in the grayness of the autumn twilight, I catch a glimpse of the roofs and walls of Santé Prison.

He talks about Bram van Velde in a tone of voice that reveals his fondness for him.

"It was horrible. He was living in dire poverty. He was living alone in his studio with his canvases, which he never showed to anyone. He had just lost his wife and he was heartbroken . . . He let me get somewhat close to him. I had to find a language, to try to reach him."

He then inquires into who I am, asks about my past.

I ask him more questions about his work and his writing.

No, he has no concept of the energy his writing contains. Nor can he imagine what these books represent to those who read them.

"I am like a mole in a tunnel."

When he started writing, he stopped reading, believing that the two activities were incompatible.

He thinks his essay on Proust is pedantic and refuses to have it translated into French.

He chose to write in French because it was a new language to him. It held an air of strangeness, permitting him to escape the reflexes inherent in the use of a mother tongue.

When he worked on *Molloy* he wrote in the afternoon, then could not sleep at night. So he forced himself to write in the morning.

He thinks there are weaknesses in his work, claims he doesn't like certain characters, who he thinks "are not right."

"Some weaknesses are necessary, but I can't forgive myself for others."

I ask him how he spends his days, and if what he has accomplished really helps him during those moments when a person stumbles, feels the ground give way under his feet.

"Sickness has been a great help to me recently."

I watch him as he stands up to reach for a book and then sits at his desk to sign it for me.

His beauty. His gravity. His concentration. His surprising timidity. The density of his silences. How intensely he brings the invisible into being.

I reflect that what makes him so impressive is, of course, his appearance, but also, and perhaps mostly, his absolute simplicity.

Simplicity in his behavior, his thought, his expression. He is essentially different. A superior man, a man who inhabits the depths, ceaselessly questioning what is most fundamental. Suddenly it is obvious to me: he is *Beckett the Inconsolable* . . .

On the doorstep we speak a while longer. He explains that he is still very tired and apologizes for not asking me to dinner. But we agree to meet again next spring, and he promises that we will have dinner together then.

He asks what my plans are during my stay. I answer that I have none, that the only reason why I came to Paris was to meet him.

"No, no, no. You should not have come all the way from Lyon to see me."

October 29, 1973

Why did I let five years go by before seeing him again? I probably did not go to Paris in the spring of 1969. Then, in the fall, as I was about to write to him, he received the Nobel Prize. Admirers, academics, old acquaintances, friends from high school or college, family members all poured in to see him from France, England, Ireland, even the United States. Beckett was overwhelmed—he even confessed to Bram van Velde that his apartment had become "a real pigsty." So, for all those years, I decided not to contact him.

We are to meet at the Closerie des Lilas. I've never set foot in this restaurant, and while waiting for him, I can't help but think of all the famous writers—Joyce, Hemingway, the Surrealists, so many others—who made this place legendary. At seven o'clock sharp, the time we agreed to meet, I see his tall figure in the distance. He is wearing dark glasses, a sheepskin jacket, a scarf in a particularly beautiful pale red.

I walk up to greet him. He looks at me silently for a few seconds, still holding my hand in his. He takes off his glasses and we go in.

He removes his jacket, tells me to sit on the bench seat while he takes a chair, which he resolutely places at an angle, so that we do not face each other. He has dark corduroy trousers on, slightly worn, and a grayish-blue turtleneck sweater.

He rolls up his sleeves. He is tan, relaxed. He smiles at me. Then he sinks into himself and thick silence settles over us.

How to begin our dialogue? Discussing things that are not of primary importance seems as impossible as assailing him head-on with the questions I am eager to ask. There is so much gravity to him that he forces calmness on you, drawing you towards the center, suddenly awakening whatever lies sleeping there, in your night.

Several minutes go by before I manage to begin the conversation.

He has just spent five weeks in Morocco. He rented a car and visited the country, went swimming, browsed the *souks*, slept on the beach . . .

Did he work a little while he was there?

"No, it was more escape than pursuit."

We discuss Bram at length. He asks me how he is doing, if he is working, what he has painted, if he still enjoys walking, if he is still just as reticent as ever. He observes regretfully that they don't see each other anymore, but I assure him that this does not prevent Bram from thinking about him often.

He mentions Bram's sister Jacoba, who is in Amsterdam struggling to make ends meet. She lives with a companion. He is younger than she is, but paralyzed. He asks if Bram knows about this. And before I answer, he goes on with a smile that clearly shows his affection:

"No, he has nothing to do with all that."

He speaks very softly, in short sentences, and sometimes his words are lost in the surrounding noise. I cannot hear him.

He has recently directed several plays. Notably in Germany. I ask if he finds this interesting.

"I do. But it's a form of distraction."

He regrets that when *Endgame* was staged in Cologne, the stage directions were disregarded and the play was set in an old folks' home. It became a caricature.

I mention how *Watt*, and then *Molloy*, met with repeated rejections. He confesses that he had given up trying to be published.

"Suzanne, my wife, is the one who insisted and found Lindon,[3] at Éditions de Minuit."

And as I try to analyze the reasons why his work might have been especially likely to meet rejection, he concludes:

"Yes, there was a kind of indecency—ontological indecency."

I mention the problem of translations, and he explains that he has to do them all himself. If he leaves it up to somebody else, he is forced to review the text word by word, and that means even more work and difficulties.

What does he think of all the essays and theses on his work? I confess to him that I often don't understand those analyses, that they seem a useless form of vivisection to me. He makes a gesture in the air with his hand, as if to brush aside something bothering him.

"Academic dementia . . ."

He talks at length about growing old. How hearing becomes more important than sight. His eyes matter much less now.

No, he does not write while taking walks. No, he does not suffer from insomnia anymore.

He is surprised to find out that I know *Fizzles*. He will send me his most recent play. It was performed in London, then in Germany, and is about to be directed and performed by Madeleine Renaud, who will simply appear as a mouth on stage.[4]

He has had to reread *Molloy* and the works that followed recently to prepare a new edition.

"How did you feel, reading them again?"

He lowers his head, stares into space, and I realize that it is not easy for him to find an answer. Suddenly his gaze and his face become like stone, and I can see that he is now very far away, that he has forgotten everything, that he has lost all notion of time and place. A fascinating sight. I am less than three feet away from him, much troubled. But I am certain that he cannot see me staring at him, and I observe him with a devouring attention.

I had forgotten how distinguished and impressive he is.

His face, where one can see hypersensitivity and energy, is just as beautiful in profile. He has the gaze of a seer, incredibly intense. His forehead is furrowed with deep wrinkles. His nose is aquiline. He has bushy and unkempt eyebrows, hollow and ill-shaven cheeks. A wide mouth, thin lips. His hair is gray, thick, and tousled.

Two, perhaps three interminable minutes pass. Then the stone comes to life and I look away. Another long moment of silence. And as I am about to ask him another question, convinced that he has lost sight of the previous one, he declares:

"I am no longer at home there."

On first reading him, I had sensed this gift of becoming completely, spontaneously absorbed in whatever requires his attention.

His breathtaking, stupefying cascades of verbal invention, his very specific way of using an image or a metaphor to reach a surprising conclusion from the most unexpected direction—all this suggests how each word he uses is filled with all his energy, all his attentiveness and inventiveness; and how he is thus capable of becoming immersed in whatever, imperiously, engages him.

Cautiously, I explain that I believe an artist's work is inconceivable without a strict ethical sense.

A long silence.

"What you say is true. But moral values are inaccessible. And they cannot be defined. In order to define them, you would have to pass a value judgment, which is impossible. That's why I could never agree with the notion of a theater of the absurd. It involves a value judgment. You cannot even speak about truth. That's what's so distressful. Paradoxically, it is through form that the artist may find some kind of a way out. By giving form to formlessness. It is only in that way, perhaps, that some underlying affirmation may be found."

I ask him about his life, how it has unfolded.

As an adolescent he did not think of becoming a writer. After finishing his studies, he entered into a university career. First he was a French lector at University College Dublin. After a year, he couldn't stand the life any longer, and he literally ran away. All the way to Germany, where he wrote his letter of resignation.

"I behaved very badly."

He came to France. Without money, without papers. President Paul Doumer had just been assassinated (this was in 1932), and foreigners were being watched very closely.

He earned a little money translating Rimbaud's "The Drunken Boat" for an American journal. To avoid being expelled, he returned to London. He considered, for a time, becoming a literary critic, and contacted several newspapers, but to no avail. He went back to his parents' house. His father was horrified. He'd had to leave school, give up studying, at the age of fifteen: one can imagine that he had trouble accepting his son's decision.

He was twenty-six and considered himself a failure. In 1933 his father died, and he was deeply affected by his death. He inherited a small sum of money and went to London, where he moved into a furnished apartment and lived in great poverty.

In 1936, following a long period of crisis, he visited Germany. By train and on foot.

In the summer of 1937 he arrived in Paris, where he settled down. He struck up a friendship with Geer and Bram van Velde, frequented Giacometti and Duchamp.

Then the war broke out. In 1942 he and his wife narrowly escaped the Gestapo, and took refuge in the village of Roussillon, in the Vaucluse.

In 1945, he went to Dublin to see his mother. Then he spent a few months in Saint-Lô working as a stockkeeper and translator in a hospital set up by the Irish Red Cross.

In 1946, he returned to Ireland, and it was there that he experienced the great upheaval that radically altered his approach to writing and his conception of narrative.

"Did this new awareness come to you gradually or in a flash?"

He speaks of a crisis, of sudden revelation.

"Until that moment I used to think I could trust knowledge, that I needed to be intellectually equipped. Then everything collapsed."

I remember his exact words:

"It was only when I understood my error that I wrote *Molloy* and what came after. I began to write things I felt."

He nods with a smile.

It happened at night. He had been wandering alone, as he often did, and found himself at the end of a jetty beaten by the waves. At that instant everything seemed to fall into place: years of doubt, of searching, questioning, failure (he was about to turn forty), suddenly became meaningful, and he saw with perfect clarity what he needed to accomplish.

"I glimpsed the world I needed to create to enable me to breathe."

He started *Molloy* while he was still with his mother. He worked on it in Paris, then in Menton, where an Irish friend[5] had loaned him his house. He completed the first part, but did not know how to continue.

He was no longer experiencing the distress of the previous years, but everything was still difficult. That is why on the first page of the manuscript of *Molloy* he wrote:

"As a last resort."

After that, until 1950, he was swept by a frenzy of creation. He wrote *Molloy, Malone Dies, Waiting for Godot, The Unnamable, Texts for Nothing,* the only works he considers to be of any value. What he wrote after 1950, he regards as mere attempts. Only in his work for the theater does he find there are perhaps a few pages slightly better than the rest.

He points out that what he is writing now has lost that feverish tone I found so impressive in *Texts For Nothing* and *The Unnamable.* He knows that what he has left in him to say is shrinking, but he feels he might just grab hold of it, or at least better circumscribe it.

We discuss the texts he has just completed, texts which are only a few pages long. He mentions those seventeenth-century Dutch paintings that functioned as memento mori. One of them depicts Saint Jerome meditating next to a death's-head. Like the painters of those canvases, he would like to be able to articulate both life and death in an extremely reduced space.

He speaks to me again of old age. But without the least bitterness. With a touch of playfulness. The peace that has come over him allows him to write more calmly. But he worries about drifting into a certain formalism. His short texts are worked out in great detail and proceed through several stages. *Imagination Dead Imagine* was preceded by eight different versions. He always moves towards reduction.

The length of a text entitled "Still," about to appear in Italian, is one page and a half.

I ask him if he still remains silent and idle for hours, observing, listening to what speaks and happens inside him. He tells me again that hearing is becoming more important to him than sight.

Again, the subject of old age, now with a sort of exhausted resignation.

I remind him that on our first meeting, he had told me how much he admired Yeats's old age.

"Yes, Yeats and Goethe . . . The active, fertile old age of great creators."

He alludes to *Fragments*, my first book.

"One senses great distress there. But now, are you doing better?"

He asks about my work, my life in Lyon. I happen to mention my *Diary*, and tell him that even though it was accepted by a publisher, it could not be published.

"It doesn't matter if you're not published. One does it to be able to breathe."

He invites me to send him some of my texts. In 1968, after our conversation, and at his express request, I had sent him thirty poems or so. He responded with a letter from which I will only quote these words: "Take distance from yourself and me."

I begin to discuss painting, and Matisse, Picasso, and Dubuffet, whose retrospective I have just seen. He acquiesces to everything I say.

He is grave, smiling, extremely present and attentive.

I feel more relaxed, and after this hour-long exchange, I feel so close to him that I have the impression of being in the presence of an old friend in whom I could confide anything. This may be why, to my surprise, I am bold enough to reveal how important encountering his work has been to my life.

Thus, in a slightly disordered fashion, allowing what is already inside me to unreel, I explain how he has taught me lucidity, torn me away from confusion, led me to focus on the essential. How what he wrote was so new, unique, that while reading him, it felt as though I were discovering language and writing for the first time. How unsettling it had been for me to find, in such alien landscapes, the very same preoccupations that had been eating away at me ever since adolescence. How I love the starkness and sharpness of his sentences, where words are laid bare, free of rhetoric and intellectuality. How I spent dozens of hours perusing, questioning, annotating his texts, in which I seemed to hear my own voice. How the silence that inhabits the pages of *Texts for Nothing* had taken me to regions of my own self where I'd never dared to venture. How his work, in a way, had destroyed me, but how it also filled me with incredible energy. How all his works describe a perfect curve, and how good it is to sense that each one of them meets some imperious necessity. How I have the utmost admiration for his exemplary life. How he alone has revealed to us what contemporary man is, unlike other writers, too concerned about keeping pace with the times. How I am grateful to him for having kept himself apart, for only the outsider can acquire a perspective capable of taking in the greatest distances and horizons. How I appreciate the way his work does not assert anything, proceeding instead by negation, then by negation of negation, causing what should be understood to flicker in that in-between space, though words never manage to capture it. How, dozens of times, I have wondered who this man could be who had written such true, such fundamental pages, who had probed so far into suffering, who had cast such an unforgiving, denuding light onto mankind and its condition. How I no longer knew if I ought to continue writing, since he seemed to have already unearthed all the possibilities in the terrain I thought I must try to explore.

I expressed all this in a jumble, in one breath, perhaps even passionately.

He stands up, all of a sudden, and asks me to excuse him.

After this brutal reminder of the reality of our situation, I watch him tilt back his head, pull his shoulders back, catch his breath. Then he takes a few steps, and finally leaves the room, stranding me in a state of great shock, confusion, and embarrassment.

Three or four interminable minutes go by. Then he returns.

An endless silence—impossible to break. Finally I manage to ask him what he is planning to do in the next few days.

"It's impossible here. I am interrupted too often. I am going to go to the country. I will spend two weeks there."

I confess to him that, once, I decided to go and see his house in the country. To walk in the surrounding fields and woods. (Arriving in the small village nearby, I noticed an elderly woman, and asked her if she knew where I could find the house of a writer named Samuel Beckett. As she was giving me directions, I began to suspect that she knew him. And without bothering to confirm my intuition, I said:

"I have the deepest admiration for this man. Would you mind telling me a little about him?"

She looked slightly surprised, then answered in a very gentle voice:

"Oh! Mr. Beckett . . . Mr. Beckett . . . He's a great man, you know . . . a great man."

I sensed that she had tried to condense everything she knew and thought about him into those few words, and did not inquire further.)

When he is at his country house—as I found out through a common friend—he writes, plays the piano, goes shopping, prepares his own meals, takes long, brisk walks, spends hours doing nothing, remains motionless, attentive to the imploring voice inside him.

"But when nothing happens, what do you do?"

"There is always something to listen for."

We meet at the Closerie des Lilas.

Again his gravity, his concentration, his self-awareness. His beauty. Deep wrinkles at the base of his nose. His hair thick, short, unkempt. A face sculpted, furrowed, spiritualized by suffering and inner tension. And yet, an impression of youth and vitality. Every time we meet, what amazes me most is his uncanny combination of silence, calm, gentleness, passivity, acquiescence, and vulnerability, on the one hand, with a quality that is ordinarily considered their opposite: exceptional energy, strength—clearly visible in his rather impressive eagle eye.

Already silence has set in, and I am not sure how to begin our conversation.

A few minutes earlier I had received a copy of the monograph that the Galerie Maeght just published on Bram van Velde.[6] I ask him if he would like to have a look. He takes it. Leafs through it, carefully looking at each reproduction, sometimes reading the same page three or four times.

We discuss Bram at great length, and he asks me several questions.

Then I ask him about his work.

"I'm always working on something. It may be long at first, but it gets shorter and shorter."

He likes what he writes less and less.

I ask him if it was difficult to renounce will, power.

"Yes, up until 1946 I tried to learn as much as possible in order to try and have some degree of power over things. Then I realized

I was following the wrong path. But perhaps all paths are wrong. Still, you have to find the wrong path that suits you best."

"Did you read the mystics?"

"Yes, when I was young. But I didn't study them in depth."

He then adds wearily:

"I have never studied anything in depth."

I conceal my astonishment. A long silence.

I resume:

"In the works of the mystics, there are dozens and dozens of sentences comparable to ones you've written. Don't you think that, leaving aside the question of religion, you share many points in common with them?"

"Yes . . . sometimes perhaps the same way of submitting to the unintelligible."

I go on, speaking about Bernard of Clairvaux and how I have found passages in his work that share the rhythm, inspiration, and incisiveness of the best pages of *The Unnamable*.

He laughs and interrupts, assuring me that he bears Clairveaux a grudge.

I know what he is alluding to, and I laugh with him.[7]

We come back to his work. He acknowledges that he has been withdrawing himself more and more from his texts.

"In the end, you no longer know who is speaking. The subject vanishes completely. That's where the identity crisis leads."

He thinks that what is demanded of the artist is that, as an individual, he vanish from his work.

I go back to *Texts For Nothing*. I paraphrase a few lines: "This teeming nothingness . . ." He smiles.

He tells me about Joyce and Proust, who both tried to create a whole world and render it in all its infinite richness. "You just have to examine their manuscripts, or the proofs they corrected," he observes. "They kept adding and adding." But *he* goes in the opposite direction, towards nothingness, always compressing his texts a little bit more.

I mention the "barrenness" of his world, both in language and devices: few characters, few peripeteia, few problems tackled, and yet, the essential is said with such force, such singularity.

He smiles and admits that, somehow, both approaches ought to be able to compromise.

"I have often wondered," I add, "how you have avoided being overwhelmed by shame."

He stops himself as he is about to answer. As he did last time, he now sinks within himself completely, and then it's as though there is nothing left alive inside him: his incredibly intense gaze now fixed and blind, his face and body like stone . . .

After several long minutes of silence, he resurfaces.

Another prolonged silence. But I feel I must go on. I tell him how surprised I am that he has been able to keep faith in writing and communication.

He too finds it surprising. He calls it a "mystery."

I move on to the universality of his work, which has enabled thousands of people throughout the world to discover previously unknown elements of themselves.

He nods.

"That too is a mystery."

He continues, but I miss some of what he is saying, he is speaking too softly.

Then we are interrupted by X—, a writer-publisher, who wants him to sign a petition.

When X— finally leaves, after pestering Beckett with his insistent demands, I know that our conversation is over.

Four or five minutes of silence as I wait for him to say he needs to go.

But then it is *he* who starts asking *me* about myself and my work.

He will go to Morocco in December, in order to escape Paris during the holidays.

I ask him about Ireland. He went there for five days in 1968 when someone died, but he does not intend to go back again. What does he think about the troubles there? He isn't interested. After a while, however, he begins to discuss the subject quite vehemently. He quotes Mitterrand saying: "Fanaticism is stupidity."

"In Ireland there aren't just two, but three, four, five kinds of fanaticism, all being torn apart by even more fanaticism."

He explains why some people are so desperate to keep Franco alive until November 25. On that day, one of Franco's supporters will be able to appoint the new head of government, whereas earlier, it would be someone from the opposite side.

"Even Goya never dreamed of such a thing."

He still visits his country house regularly, and spends two to three weeks there at a time. In the morning he writes. In the afternoon he works around the house, strolls in the field, or drives to more secluded spots where he takes walks.

"Don't you get lonely?"

He makes a surprised gesture.

"No, no. Not at all. On the contrary. Though when I was younger, I wouldn't have been able to stand it."

He speaks enthusiastically about the silence there. He loves being able to follow the course of the sun from sunrise to sunset.

Remembering what X— was saying a few minutes ago, he talks about the desire for literary fame. He mentions Van Gogh . . .

"When you think that he never sold a single canvas—"

"Has Van Gogh been very important to you?"

The intensity of his stare makes me realize that my question has hit very close to home

He almost answers me two or three times, but finally does not. Protracted silence. The contact between us has been broken, since X—'s interruption. When we leave, I cannot help but feel frustrated and disappointed.

November 11, 1977

Late morning. I am waiting for him at the bar of a grand hotel opposite his apartment. On my way there, I ran into Mrs. Beckett, who was going shopping.

Japanese tourists are sitting at neighboring tables, and the place is quite noisy. I retreat into thoughts of the silence Beckett needs, the silence I like to feel behind his words, and am reminded of an anecdote that Beckett had once told Bram van Velde—according to Van Velde—with a rather grim look on his face.

A writer is sitting at his desk facing an open window. Suddenly, he hears a voice blaring from the concierge's radio, right beneath his window.

After several minutes the writer loses his patience and runs to the window, screaming, "I'm going to break that radio!"

Contritely, the concierge begs, "But sir, my radio is all I have in life."

To which the writer replies, "Well, in that case, forget I said anything."

Beckett arrives. He is relaxed, and the conversation begins quite easily.

He inquires into Bram van Velde's health, his work, how he's reacting to the terrible blow he recently suffered.[8] He asks if Van Velde still enjoys taking walks. If he still pronounces those trenchant aphorisms he is known for. Did he take his brother's death very badly? He is surprised that both men had let so many years go by without seeing each other. I try to explain why.

"Still," he concludes—and I can feel both sadness and disbelief in his voice—"Still . . . Two brothers . . ."

He hadn't seen Geer the last few years, but he still likes his work, and he has kept the two paintings of his he bought before the war.

Geer's wife phoned him a little while ago. Supposedly Geer had tried to call Beckett before he died.

He has just spent three weeks in his country house. He took walks, played the piano often, read a little. He has been reading Heine's last poems, and he tells me that they are like lamentations. But he prefers doing nothing. Spending hours looking out the window. He is particularly fond of the silence. He also describes the sound of cartloads of beetroots as they pass his house.

But how can he endure the passage of time?

"It doesn't weigh on me. I even think that the days go by too quickly. It amazes me. When I was younger, I couldn't have stood being alone for so many days."

He adds with a smile:

"I sometimes count my own steps as I walk."

"What have you been working on lately?"

"Last night I couldn't get to sleep for a long time, so I thought up a play. It would last one minute."

He becomes animated, all at once, changes the position of his chair to face me, and pushes aside our drinking glasses, his lighter, and the metal box holding his small cigars.

"One human being, standing silent, motionless. Slightly to the rear, almost offstage." He points to a place on the table, which stands for the stage. "Everything takes place in twilight. Someone else enters. He steps forward. Slowly. He notices the character standing motionless. He stops in wonder.

"'Are you waiting for someone?'

"The other one shakes his head no.

"'For something?'

"Same answer.

"After a few seconds he continues on his way.

"As he does, the other one asks:

"'Where are you going?'

"'I don't know.'"

After a while he concludes with a smile:

"I should submit it somewhere, perhaps."

We discuss *Footfalls*, his latest play. He explains the importance of human steps, of our steps on the earth.

"Always that back-and-forth movement . . ." He acts out with his fingers the pacing of a prisoner in his cell, of an animal in its cage. "That's something Bram knows all about, the sound of those steps—"

Images occur to me, and I mention his work. His global view of the whole. In his latest stories and plays, all unusually brief, the entire human condition is expressed in very few words: waiting, distress, hope, love, death . . . He is extremely attentive to concreteness, he grasps the smallest detail, and at the same time his eye, fixed on Sirius, can embrace the whole.

"Yes," he says, nodding . . . "You must be here," he says, pointing towards the table, "and also," pointing his index finger upward, "millions of light-years away. All at the same time . . ."

A long silence.

"The fall of a leaf and the fall of Satan: it's all the same."

He laughs heartily; his whole face laughs:

"Wonderful, isn't it? The same thing."

Long silence.

"But how to express it ? There is no personal pronoun . . . *I, he, we* . . . nothing really works."

Silence.

"Everything in this damned world calls for indignation . . . But as far as work goes . . . What can be said? Nothing is sayable."

I try to pinpoint the singularity of his work. I observe that over the last four centuries, man seems to have endeavored to give a reassuring and gratifying image of himself. It is precisely this image that Beckett has been trying to tear apart.

He points out that Leopardi, Schopenhauer, and a few others preceded him along the way.

I go on with my argument.

"Yes," he admits, "perhaps with them there was still hope for an answer, for a solution. Not with me."

I add that by giving up positive wording, he has chosen to surrender himself to an approach based on negation.

He corrects me:

"Negation is not possible. Nor affirmation. It is absurd to say that it is absurd. That's still passing a value judgment. There can be no protest, no agreement."

Then, after a long pause:

"One must stand where there is no pronoun, no solution, no reaction, no tenable position . . . That's what makes work so diabolically difficult."

I ask him what he is working on.

He is currently writing in English, a language which has now become foreign to him. But he then needs to translate it back into French, which is additional work that he would gladly avoid: he does not like going back to a text that he has already taken as far as it could go.

Madeleine Renaud performed *Not I* in Japan, and it was a real success. He cannot understand why his work is so well received over there.

We talk about Ireland, about his family.

Did his closest relatives have any knowledge of what he wrote? No. Neither his father, who died in 1933, nor his mother, who died in 1950, nor his brother, who died in 1954 (and who disapproved of his commitment to writing) ever read a single page by him.

"Were you able to do away with the influence of religion?"

"In my outward behavior, probably . . . But as for the rest . . ."

He inquires into my work. I answer, and again question him about his own.

He tells me laughingly that he has just completed some short poems in regular verse, which he calls *Mirlitonnades* (doggerel verses). I venture to ask him if he would consent to send something to a friend of mine who is starting a journal, and he is kind enough to accept.

(A few days later, my friend received this brief poem taken from *Mirlitonnades*:

> glimmers edges
> of the shuttle
> one more step go out
> half-turn reshimmer
>
> halt rather
> far from both
> at home without self
> or them[9]

What was said to me during our meeting certainly helped me elucidate these rather elliptical lines.)

I speak to him of Hölderlin. He is especially fond of his "mad" poems, but he confesses that entire pages leave him cold. Six to eight years ago, when he was in Stuttgart for some television work, he visited the tower in Tübingen where Hölderlin spent the last thirty years or so of his life, a prisoner of his madness.

I ask him more questions about what he has read. Yes, a great deal of Shakespeare. And the Bible, especially when he was young. He reminds me that his family was Protestant, and he adds that Protestants are very keen on the Old Testament. He used to own an English Bible in a translation dating back to 1610. The text was packed with mistakes, but extremely beautiful.

I mention the prophets, Isaiah, Jeremiah, Amos . . .

He nods and whispers pensively:

"Job . . ."

I allude to the mystics, Saint John of the Cross, Meister Eckhart, Ruysbroeck . . . I ask him if he ever rereads them, once in a while—if he likes what emanates from their writings.

"Yes . . . I like . . . I like their . . . their illogicality . . . their burning illogicality—the flame . . . the flame . . . which consumes all our filthy logic . . ."

Conversations with Bram van Velde

Translated by Janey Tucker,
Morgaine Reinl, and Aude Jeanson

splashes waste rigor
giving up

impatience
        tension
                remorse

a form seeks
to become apparent
hesitates asserts itself
gives in to uncertainty
pulls itself together again
changes
structures itself

and suddenly the structure
falls apart
disappears
reappears as another
sketches out *the face*
of what does not have
a face
disappears again
reappears again
        building
        a new space

a new rhythm

demanding to be looked at
differently

the act of painting
is experienced as
impossible

it is overcome
by the conscience
of its own vanity

life
        that materializes
life
        that vanishes
a proclamation
that's denied
as soon as
it's made

a point is reached
where nothing can be said

where the need to go beyond
becomes apparent

a need to break
the silence

venturing to
express oneself
at all costs

in order to show
what cannot be
seen

to represent
what could not
be said

a basic
energy

a raw desire
to live

sometimes
one can manage to glimpse
the magnificence
of this circle

and streams of energy

      emptiness
      and smooth
      shapes

      a tight heavy

texture

verging
on implosion

run through the painting
flow over it

follow the movements
of a large wide form
        kept open
        by tensions
        that will never
        cease

and once again
the structure
falls apart

gives rise
to another

and both of them
fit into each other
become entangled
upset
the eye

draw an obvious troubled
image

changing

mysterious

and the bright colors
harsh light subtle
struggle change

are glorified

are dulled

let an unexpected
transparency
filter through

and the painting
like a scream

a center
without a center

defeated

an offer
never quite made

the painting tells
the story
of its own genesis

radiates
the light
of its birth
with subtlety

of birth
of what gave it birth

but also
brings to the fore the portrait
of this sunken
man

frightened   determined

condemned to something that can never cease
a hatred of the center

and who used to sign
                    and does not sign any longer
                                        B V V

First meeting with Bram van Velde. I arrive at 6 P.M. at the house of Jacques Putman, a friend who has, I believe, spent a lot of time with him, and who is busy trying to gain recognition for his work via articles, books, and exhibitions.[1] I don't know what sort of person the painter is and I'm afraid he'll be annoyed by my visit and give me a cool reception. I am surprised to find him a remarkably shy person, quite overwhelmed that a stranger has come to talk to him about his painting. I sit down. He offers me a drink but finds it hard to meet my eye and keeps on getting up and sitting down again. His attitude makes me even more nervous and I can hardly manage to get out a couple of halting questions. To escape the creeping embarrassment of the situation and to break our near-silent confrontation, he suggests we go out for a walk. Outside, freed of the necessity of looking at each other, we begin to talk. A moment later, the ice is broken and he has invited me out to dinner. When I take my leave of him, it is past eleven o' clock.

I managed to get him to talk about himself. He told me that he left Holland at the age of twenty-five and has never returned, apart from two or three years ago when there was a retrospective of his work at the Stedelijk Museum in Amsterdam.[2] He hasn't seen his family since. His brother Geer,[3] also a painter, lives in Paris but he has lost touch with him in recent years. His sister Jacoba[4] is a writer and lives in Amsterdam. He himself painted in absolute isolation up to the age of fifty and his first exhibition[5] was a disaster. From the age of twenty-five he devoted himself entirely to his painting, and consequently lived for thirty years in great poverty. In 1940, when he had reached the end of his tether and could take no more, he turned to Samuel Beckett, whom he had met four years earlier. For the first time, somebody understood his paintings, his silent struggle, his obstinate determination to hold out at the extreme limit of creative possibility. (Nobody was better equipped than Beckett to accept and appreciate his kind of painting. Perhaps it actually cast light on he himself, and on what he was preparing to write.)

He spoke of Beckett to me in wonderful terms. *He is so generous,* he told me, *so kind. So intelligent, so understanding, so sympathetic. He knows, without trying, exactly what to say to appeal to your very essence. When you see him, you feel that he encompasses the whole of life; you understand that human existence is one huge, painful adventure.*

I reminded him that he had once told the sculptor Maxime Descombin that *painting is searching for the countenance of that which has no countenance,* and that *painting is man facing his downfall . . .* His words had seemed extraordinarily accurate to Descombin and, as I quote them to Van Velde, he misunderstands and believes them to be Descombin's, declaring that they are indeed irrefutable and absolutely represent the artistic process. When I make it clear that the source of the words was not in fact Descombin but Van Velde himself, he looks away, overcome by embarrassment. It was then I realized that he takes self-renunciation so far that he is determined to efface from his memory anything that he may himself have discovered and put into words, wishing to be consistently and absolutely transparent in relation to himself and to his painting. In fact, you get the feeling that he is exceedingly sensitive, vulnerable, and defenseless, fearful of life and of people. He frequently fails to repress a nervous smile. But when he is thinking, his features are transformed: they take on an expression of extraordinary acuity, and his face becomes all tension and energy.

I ask him how he managed to survive financially during the period of thirty years in which he devoted himself to his painting but sold nothing. *I never begged*, he told me, *but in that respect I have always believed in miracles*. No doubt his nobility of spirit and resignation to his fate were such that those who crossed his path were impressed and helped him without being asked. I ask him again if those years hadn't been terrible and suggest that it must have required something close to heroism to survive them. He shrugs. *No*, he says, *it wasn't all terrible. There were good times too. And anyway, you know, there's no choice. I wasn't free to live any other way.*

In three days' time, a major exhibition of his work is due to open in New York, after which it will tour other big museums in the United States.[6] He is astonished and amused by this event, of which he is the author but from which he feels completely detached.

He has just arrived from Geneva, where he's been living, I believe, for the last two years. He will soon be seventy. He has no family, no home, no studio. Utterly alone. Utterly dispossessed. Marvelously free, serene, and lacerated. Before leaving, I ask him what he does when he's not painting. *I am always about to*, he replies, *I am just waiting and getting ready*.

November 9, 1965

Lunch alone with Bram van Velde at Jacques Putman's house. An intense experience. Such life and youthfulness in the man. But you also feel that he is terribly agonized and dispossessed. When he is thinking, his eyes take on an unbearable brilliance. It is as if they cease to exist as matter and become entirely subsumed into their own expression.

He is there but not there, in the grip of his obsessions. So no conversation. Silence. Long periods of silence. His eyes are absent, incandescent; his face takes on a sudden acuity or lights up in a smile of wonder or disbelief. Then a sentence is spoken, and continues to reverberate in the prolonged silence.

"It is terrible to live without power over words.

"A painter is someone who can't use words. His only escape is to be a seer.

"No, I mustn't grumble. It's extraordinary enough to escape the massacre.

"It's thanks to people like Beckett that things don't collapse.

"He's a great man. He has never evaded anything."

And when I suggest that life must sometimes be terrible for those who refuse all evasion:

"Yes, of course it is. But he is so above it all that he doesn't let it show.

"It's both terrible and wonderful, because it is true, because it is life itself.

"Painting is so stupid, so simple. I paint to get out of the trough. I paint my misery.

"Artists don't live in the everyday world. That's why people think they're an odd bunch.

"The most difficult thing is when you can't do anything. When you just have to wait."

I suggest that painters are better off than writers, because they are more intuitive, more instinctive, less at risk of being fettered by the intellect and by the concepts, words, and conventions of an acquired utilitarian language.

He replies, with an amused and mischievous smile:

"Yes of course, painters get further because they are stupider."

I also say that modern artists seem to me to bear new responsibilities, that they have a new role in that they are now almost alone in devoting their lives to a quest for the meaning of life, and that since all forms of spirituality have dried up they are discovering their true role. He interrupts me and says with great gentleness, as if stating the obvious:

"They are the prophets, the martyrs."

After a lengthy pause, I refer to a painter who also writes and dabbles in philosophy.

"He's lucky," he retorts. "He's got words. He doesn't need to paint any more."

He is busy rereading *Death on the Installment Plan*.[7]

During this meeting we also talk about sculpture. He admits that, in general, it has meant little to him, but says that he has, twice in his life—once in Paris and once in Holland—been very struck by a piece of sculpture, and that on each occasion it turned out to be by Wotruba.

The walls of the large living room in which we sit are hung with several of his paintings, dating from different periods. I look at them. He looks with me. He neither admires them nor affects to underestimate them, nor does he hasten to explain them to me or to stress that he has progressed further since then. He simply gazes at them, smiling, shaking his head, lost in wonder at the fact that they are his own brainchildren.

After the meal he apologizes for having to leave me. He has to go and work and I accompany him in the direction of his studio. In the street, I notice that he is ill at ease, afraid of the traffic. We pass through the Jardin du Luxembourg. I ask how many canvases he has painted since my last visit in October:

"Three." Then, after a lengthy pause: "I couldn't do any more."

He smiles apologetically.

"And, are you pleased with them?"

"Oh . . . yes . . . yes . . . You know, they're always just as wretched."

It's a beautiful day and I suggest we sit down for a moment. We sit in silence. Long, long minutes of silence. Then we part.

October 31, 1966

Yesterday I met Bram van Velde in Geneva. I can't describe the atmosphere of this encounter, or put into words what I feel in his presence, the rush of new life within me in response to what he says.

Such an honest, unpretentious man, with such an astonishing intensity of life and acuity of mind about him. I have already said that it is impossible to hold a normal conversation with him, and that the exchange takes place more by way of silences than through words (so that, even if you speak sparingly, it feels like grandiloquence). He smiles and laughs frequently—in fact, he shakes with laughter—but silently, modestly, ill at ease and amazed at the thoughts forming in his own mind (but which he will not necessarily communicate to you, either because it doesn't occur to him to do so or because he breaks off in mid-sentence), himself amazed to discover what he is saying, and amazed yet again at having to use such strange words, so alien to the thoughts they are trying to express. I ask him questions and after some little lapse of time he replies with an abrupt phrase, like a flash of lightning, producing sudden illumination and intensifying the sense of luminosity already created by his eyes.

A few phrases recalled at random:

"The most difficult thing is not to want anything.

"Everything has to end before it can begin.

"You experience some funny things in your life.

"It's terrible, all that. But you can only laugh about it.

"You're in constant danger of being destroyed

"I can't say anything. There are no words.

"The important thing is to be nothing.

"The less you think, the better it is.

"The more you know, the less you are.

"No, I never knew either Mondrian or Kandinsky. I didn't know what they were doing. You can't be everywhere.

"The beauty other people create is not for the artist. Artists have to live alone.

"Everyone cheats. Only artists don't. They don't fool people and they aren't fooled. They're outside all that. Nobody can understand them.

"Painting is an eye, a blinded eye that continues to see, and sees what blinds it.

"This tiny little thing, which is nothing, which dominates life."

He has given me a catalogue and together we study a reproduction in it of one of the most impressive canvases he has ever painted. The exact opposite of a painting claiming to be a masterpiece. The very image of laceration. The search for a glimmer of light in the hopeless tangle of things, the need to organize chaos, the refusal of any false order. It is the literal transcription of the state of dilapidation into which the spirit is often plunged, when at the very point of no return the exultant life force intervenes and can hurl it back to the opposite extreme.

"That's life," he explains, "space turned into life. Every living person shares in this condition. It cannot be otherwise."

On the subject of Beckett, about whom he talks to me each time with eager devotion:

"He sees himself as dead and he is more alive than anyone else.

"He is dispossessed and he has this frightening strength. Both are necessary."

A moment later, I make ironical mention of Picasso:

"Picasso," he guffaws . . . And, shaking with silent laughter, full of comical candor: "The master . . . being a master . . . I don't search, I find . . . the master, the mastery . . . Producing, producing . . . He only knows how to work, can't do anything else. What lost souls!

"The great risk is producing for its own sake. You must never force things. You just have to wait."

As for himself, in fifty years of creative life he has painted some three hundred canvases and gouaches. I know that for a long time life was hard. Recently, in Lyon, I had the opportunity to talk to a woman who had met him after the war. She told me that at that time he was living in a garage, wrestling with appalling poverty. I try to get him to talk about those years, but he can't. I understand. Freeing himself of all potential impediments. The spirit entirely given over to its struggle.

December 31, 1966

I visit Bram van Velde.

"No, I haven't been working. I like to get out walking, and in this weather I can't. Painting needs space to live and in the winter I don't have the space. And anyway, my mind is on Turin." (Where a retrospective of his work is being held at the museum.)[8]

"In the first piece that Beckett wrote about me, he never once used the word color. That was important. I was struck by it.

"To be true, you have to take the plunge, to touch bottom. But most people want to be in control. They fear the worst. You can't control anything. What you have to do is let yourself be taken over.

"I celebrate my misery. My pictures are celebrations of misery.

"Art has never been in serious jeopardy.

"Many painters produce one painting after another, for absolutely no good reason at all.

"All the paintings I have made, I was compelled to make. You must never force yourself.

"They make you and you have no say in it. It's Godot all the time. A chain around your neck and the whip cracking behind you.

"Yes, I abandoned everything. Painting required it. It was all or nothing.

"Painting is being alive. Through my painting, I beat back this world that stops us living and where we are in constant danger of being destroyed."

From what he tells me about his exhibition, I realize that he viewed it with eyes as fresh and innocent as those of the visitors. In him, the past is obliterated. Totally focused on the future. I tell him that the best introduction would have been something written by himself, or a few of his thoughts. He bursts out laughing. I think that, in his concern for total humility, he refuses to assist his work in any way, to help people approach it, to defend it or to cast light on it. *No*, he continues, *you have to know when to keep silent.* And I am immediately reminded of Braque's aphorism: "Evidence exhausts the truth."

April 2, 1967

I visit Bram van Velde.

"Painting is an aid to vision. It turns life, the complexity of life, into something visible. It reveals things that we don't know how to see."

Of a painter we have just been discussing: "What he's looking for is to produce a good picture. What I'm looking for is painting, life.

"Mondrian? His mind was too subtle. He worked in the light. I work in the darkness.

"Mondrian is the Buddha of painting. I saw him once. You wondered how a man could radiate such charisma.

"These production-line painters.

"It's terrible being a painter.

"I am trying to see, when everything in this world conspires to prevent us from seeing.

"For the artist, it's all or nothing. If it's not all, then it's nothing.

"I paint the impossibility of painting.

"In this world that destroys me, the only thing I can do is to live my weakness. That weakness is my only strength.

"The artist is living a secret that he has to make manifest.

"I can't say or explain anything. Pictures don't come from your head but from life.

"No, I haven't produced anything, so I've been working hard.

"I am always looking for life. All that escapes thought or will-power.

"When you cross any border"—from where we were walking we could see the customs officials and their post—"there is always an uneasy moment when you feel yourself automatically an enemy. Artists don't belong to any group or country.

"These painters who know how to produce a painting according to the rules and theories.

"When you are living the truth, the world no longer exists, events become unimportant. But the way of truth is not easy.

"If you're on the side of truth, you have no power. That's why you are always defeated. The power, all the power, is on the side of the world.

"Life is frightening.

"I have been completely absorbed in my adventure. No country, no family, no ties. I didn't exist anymore. I just had to press on.

"When you know, you lose everything, you can't go on."

We talk at length about Beckett.

"His mind has never flinched. Nothing has ever frightened him.

"I have no defenses, I am laughable, I sometimes feel I am grotesque. But he's got the weapons you need to disarm malice. He makes himself unassailable.

"Somebody who has taken account of error can't be wrong. Everything he says is true.

"Despite all that happens to him (his fame), he's still on the side of truth."

It is a fine spring day and we are sitting out on the lawn in front of the house.

"Look," he says, pointing skyward. "See how beautiful it is."

A sparrow hawk is circling above us and Bram confides to me that he can never see one on the wing without being moved by the sight. How well I understand. I spend hours tramping the hills around my village watching the hawks soaring above me. I search my memory for a moment and am pleased to be able to reel off a passage which struck me particularly in *Malone Dies*:

> But he loved the flight of the hawk and could distinguish it from all others. He would stand rapt, gazing at the long pernings, the quivering poise, the wings lifted for the plummet drop, the wild reascent, fascinated by such extremes of need, of pride, of patience and solitude.[9]

"Beckett sees red if you swat a fly when he's around. But he doesn't forget that the hawk would die of hunger if it stayed sitting on its branch.

"All these exhibitions . . . People put out their hands to you, and when you try to take them, there's nobody there."

His childlike astonishment in the face of this mystery that possesses him, in the face of these evident truths that spring from his lips and by which he is the first to be surprised, in the face of this world where he feels he has no place. In his presence, everything becomes bizarre.

A word, a gust of silent laughter, reveals with extraordinary acuteness the grotesque or absurd or inhuman aspect of some feature of life or of our times. Often, I feel as if he is a visitor from another world. I say so and he agrees. Then, a few seconds later:

"*I do see this world. But my hands are tied, and that's why it frightens me.*"

Yesterday, back from a tour of Switzerland with M.L. and Mysou, we spent the evening with Madeleine[10] and Bram. Once again impressed by his concentration, his intensity, by the acuity of his expression. Particularly when we were looking at the pictures he has painted this summer. M.L. and Mysou were struck by his good looks and distinction.

During the meal, and against all expectations, he appeared relaxed and on-form; he amused us with several anecdotes and talked about Worpswede, the little village in northern Germany where he lived between 1922 and 1925. He became very emotional at that point, on the verge of tears. But since it's impossible to reproduce the way he speaks—so remarkable, even though so simple and direct—his prolonged silences, his smiles, his reticence, the quality of his humor, his abrupt utterances and sudden changes of expression, I prefer to record here only what I remember.

Gazing at the paintings he has just finished:

"Life is so difficult to catch.

"Each time it's an attempt to get there. To get to see. To get to where you can see.

"Through painting I try to get closer to nothingness, to the void.

"The artist is the bearer of life.

"Life is wrecked by living.

"Dead days are more numerous than live ones."

At table, I ask him about some painters whose work we have just seen in the major Swiss museums.

"X? Well, yes . . . But there's nothing revolutionary about him. He doesn't get beyond just painting.

"Y? He was an absolute fraud. He ended up playing a part and identifying with his own idea of himself. He didn't even know he was doing it, he couldn't know. He was a real artist though.

"Z? He's a crime . . . a criminal . . . You can't be a painter with an electronic brain in your head. Oh, intellect . . . a climbing iron to help you up. Painting's a different thing altogether.

"Painters who get a taste of success go quite mad. They are as corrupt as a Rockefeller. Van Gogh was the purest and he never sold one painting. He had to commit suicide. X is rolling in it. He's the madman.

"Ah! Baudelaire . . . He used to be enormously important to me. It's thanks to him that I was able to get through the war. A true, loyal mind without hypocrisy. The most universal spirit. The greatest Frenchman. I have always been much less interested in painters." (And I am all the more surprised to hear this because it is painters rather than writers who have helped me discover my own deepest intuitions.)

Inevitably, we talk about Beckett, and Bram tells us that while reading *Endgame* he has sometimes thought he recognized the tone and odd fragments of their conversations. And suddenly, fixing me with his intense stare, arm outstretched, finger pointing at me, he declares:

"Now he's dying to go and see Beckett. But he's scared, he won't go."

And after a pause:

"But why don't you go and see him? Be courageous. There's no reason why he should refuse to talk to somebody who has something to say to him.

"The world is getting sicker and sicker. More and more frightening. Tomorrow, they'll be going to the moon. But the earth's a disaster area.

"Of course, painting is ridiculous. But it's the only way I've got to get closer to life.

"I paint gouaches when I haven't the strength to tackle oils.

"An artist's life is all very fine and moving. But only in retrospect. In books.

"Artists who are the defenders of true life become phonies. That's the perfidious thing about this world. Society turns anyone with a bit of life inside them into a medical case.

"I don't like talking. I don't like people talking to me. Painting is silence.

"To express nothingness, misery.

"You have to keep on to the end without giving in.

"A painter is somebody who sees. I paint the moment when I set out, when I set out to see. And it's the same thing for the viewer. When he approaches the canvas, he is advancing towards an encounter. The encounter with vision.

"You can't paint everything, as many people think.

"I am on the side of weakness.

"Art. To avoid being ground down"

December 28, 1967

Passing two children at play:

"They don't know about the drama yet.

"Words, they're just noise. Even little children get taught to make a noise.

"The road to success is the path to perdition.

"The artist has no role. He is absent.

"For the most part, his story is absurd.

"It is through misery that I have gotten closer to *life*.

"A phony artist is the worst kind of criminal.

"To have a lasting vision.

"There's a perpetual duel going on between the world of the spirit and the world of things. Although the one only has meaning in relation to the other.

"I don't really understand sculpture. It doesn't seem to allow for experiment.

"During the war, I found it impossible to paint. Other people went on as if nothing was happening. Nobody else was surprised at them, but I could never understand it.

"Most people's lives are governed by willpower. An artist is someone who has no will.

"To be nothing. Just nothing. It's a frightening experience. You have to let go of everything.

"Art is taking risks.

"A sincere attempt to achieve the impossible, the unknown.

"If one were always to remain in that zone, it would be phony.

"A canvas is a great occasion. But there are painters who latch onto a recipe and imagine that that can produce great occasions.

"I am in the void. Nothing to hang on to.

"Waiting for the truth.

"Van Gogh . . . Fascinating. The fragility of that strong spirit.

"There is always doubt. There's nothing you can get hold of.

"It's so rare, someone who sees.

"Each of my paintings is a cycle. It's like existence, life. They are always in motion. If they were fixed and static, they would be false.

"Society rejects the artist. I am constantly afraid."

Following some talk about a poet:

"Yes, it's something of a game he's playing. I have always had doubts, but never where play is concerned.

"When you get to the bottom, you discover that there is no room for pride. That's what I paint."

April 13, 1968

We go out for a walk. Long silences, during which I have all the time in the world to hone my questions. Questions I have already asked him often enough, and to which I can more or less foresee the answers. But I ask them again anyway, fearing at times to be a nuisance, but knowing that the answers that spring from his lips will always be richer, more comprehensive, or more remarkable than any I could ever imagine.

"Painting doesn't interest me.

"What I paint is beyond painting.

"I am powerless, helpless. Each time, it's a leap in the dark. A deliberate encounter with the unknown.

"People don't know what it's like at times, having to cover a surface with colors.

"I don't set out to speak a comprehensible language. But my language is authentic.

"In this world, you have to be a bit mad to be an artist. But there are plenty of artists who are pretending to be mad.

"Each painting contains so much suffering.

"When I look back at a recent painting, I can hardly bear the suffering in it.

"Each painting is linked to a fundamental drama.

"I have to try to see where seeing is no longer possible, where visibility is gone.

"Yes, perhaps there's some enjoyment in it too, somewhere."

A week ago, I met Beckett. On the wall behind me was a painting by Bram. It faces Beckett's desk, so that he sees it when he's working. I was struck by the affection and admiration he bears Bram and by the fervor with which he talks about him:

"It was horrible. He was living in dire poverty. He was living alone in his studio with his canvases, which he never showed to anyone. He had just lost his wife and he was heartbroken . . . He let me get somewhat close to him. I had to find a language, to try to reach him."

Today, walking with Bram beside the Lake, I tell him about this meeting.

"I am glad you have met him. You have to see him . . . It's a unique experience."

Then, editing where necessary but being careful not to distort anything, I recount what Beckett told me about him.

"Yes, in me he found total despair."

A winter's day, gray and cheerless. Bram is gloomy, his thoughts elsewhere. I talk to him about Van Gogh. About Freundlich, and how I learned only a few days ago just what a remarkable man he was.

"Doubt is at the root. Since Van Gogh, doubt has increased. Now, pain is the only source.

"Freundlich . . . He was another martyr to art.

"When there is nothing, you begin to see a cycle.

"Life is one huge massacre.

"When the worst is avoided, something's wrong somewhere."

April 1, 1969

We are walking down a narrow country road. There are peasants at work in the fields.

"You must feel very far removed from these people," I suggest.

"I see it all ... With a kind of panic. But somehow it all comes together again and I feel that I am not so very different from them.

"Yes, I have always lived a very solitary life.

"I am a primitive being.

"You have to submit.

"It's so strange, this need to see and make others see.

"Everything has to happen in isolation from the will, the intellect. You have to let the unknown well up ...

"If it weren't for this spark (his need to be, to see, and to make others see), it would all be just dust. But in the end there are plenty of people who are drawn towards that spark.

"If Beckett tells you he's not free and can't see you, it's because he really can't. You can be sure of that. He has such respect for life.

"Painting ... Misery and splendor ...

"I can't talk about what goes on inside me. And anyway words are so threadbare.

"Life is exhausting, isn't it? Often you just can't do it, you can't go on.

"We are all going under. But we daren't admit it to ourselves.

"All my life, what has struck me most has been the immense cowardice of the way we live our lives. A truly infinite cowardice."

"Every phrase that Beckett writes is something he has somehow experienced. There's never anything cerebral about him.

"He has the means to succor those in need of comfort. And he does so whenever he can. He is so kind.

"You haven't got two eyes, you've got a thousand.

"The most fantastic thing is that everything happens in isolation from the will. Wanting doesn't come into it.

"Through wanting to transcend (to transcend himself, to transcend others), he (a writer whom we have just been discussing) has ended up leaving life behind.

"French painting . . . So often it lacks a certain savagery.

"So many artists end up playing a part, identifying with a fictional character. They are no longer part of the adventure."

I tell him about a boy I know who admires writers and painters who willfully go to extremes. His answer is immediate:

"It just shows how far his head is from his eyes."

We discuss the canvas he is working on:

"As you've seen, I am still a long way from . . . But I'm trying to get closer to it. Sometimes that's all you can hope for. But the process of getting closer obviously has something sacred about it.

"We are always two people. One living and one dead. And the two are in constant conflict.

"This illumination you sometimes achieve isn't something you can hang on to. In fact, you lose it again right away. Each time, you have to set out to look for it again.

"It is difficult to keep the whole thing in focus."

December 27, 1969

> I am talking about everything in these paintings that is unreasoned, artless, uncontrived, and unfinished. [. . .] This kind of categorical carelessness or haughty negligence, this disdainful use of sovereign resources, which so well translates [. . .] the urgency and primacy of the artist's vision.

These are two sentences from "La peinture des van Velde ou le monde et le pantaloon," so far as I know the first thing Beckett wrote about Bram.[11] A trenchant piece of writing, of eminently Beckettian singularity. Bram hadn't even kept a copy of it. A literary friend of mine procured it for me and I have typed it out and passed it on to him.

After the meal, we go out for a walk. Bram doesn't like the winter. He can't work. He is gloomy, and even less inclined to talk than usual.

"Colors are like music. Liberty, liberty, invention.

"Each painting represents a moment when you could do it, when you had the strength.

"They cheat to avoid the worst.

"It is only by accepting the worst that you can have anything to say.

"There must be no softening of the truth.

"A painting is an act, an adventure, an invention.

"For me, this (painting) has been vital."

Bram lost in his depths, desperately bent on excavating his soul, his dazzling blue eyes, fixed and intense, turned inwards. Or Bram present, quivering with fright.

"At exhibition openings, I feel as if I'm being assailed on every side. Like those jellyfish on the beach. Children stab them with their sticks without realizing that they are living creatures.

"A painting has nothing to do with rational thought.

"The invisible life depicted on the canvas is more real than what people regard as real life.

"Painting comes from so far away, it's difficult to see it clearly.

"I never try to know.

"The mistake so many artists make is to believe that this adventure is a matter of willpower.

"To be completely alone and defenseless all the time is a terrible thing. You have to be incredibly brave.

"Even solitude is not something you can will. You put up with it. That's all you can do.

"Everything I've painted is the revelation of a truth. And therefore inexhaustible.

"Only painting could take charge of my adventure.

"I put all my energy into my painting. I have no strength left over for anything else."

Once again, I try to get him to talk about his childhood. In vain. Again I discover that for him the past is dead and buried; it holds no interest. The only answer I get is:

"I was a little savage."

July 16, 1970

He tells me about their visit to Italy:

"Deep down, you're even more anguished. But you pretend there's nothing wrong. In Naples, you see all those wretched people struggling to survive from day to day, and then you feel the full horror of life."

A while ago he saw Beckett again. He found him gloomy, tired, aged. After embracing:

Bram: "We never see each other anymore."

Beckett: "Only physically."

He talks again about Beckett's extraordinary sensitivity:

"In him, the word becomes life."

I bring up the subject of Rothko's suicide.

"Perhaps he couldn't stand real life anymore.

"X . . . He's more of an establishment figure than a seeker.

"Y . . . He's limited though. Safe. Always the same picture. Me, I never know where I'm going.

"The hardest thing is to work blind.

"In the normal way, nothing is possible, but the artist creates possibilities where almost none exist.

"It's because artists are defenseless that they have such power.

"If you're engaged in the adventure, you can't compromise.

"There is nothing but doubt and hesitation. And yet, you're gripped by a compulsion that drives you on."

I talk about the moments of power and intensity, when vision is present.

"Of course. But they are so brief. Most of the time, you're just in a vacuum, waiting."

Once again, at the risk of annoying him, I ask him about Mondrian.

"Perhaps he was too faithful to a single discovery. And perhaps that kind of painting was right for the period. But now peace and harmony are no longer possible. There is only anguish."

We are surrounded by fields of wheat. I talk about Van Gogh.

"Van Gogh? . . . In this world of petty calculations, he was too intense. He frightened people. They cast him out."

He has been working and he is relaxed. He says again how much he prefers the summer, when he is always less anguished than during the winter.

I tell him that my *Journal* is going to be published and that I have accepted the editor's suggestion that it should be issued anonymously.

"I have experienced the same problem. That's why I have stopped signing my paintings. You can't put a name on something that transcends the individual.

"To achieve anything at all, you have to be nothing."

August 24, 1970

Bram is relaxed, grave, and sprightly. He keeps calling me *tu*[12] and talks with astounding vivaciousness, acuity, and youthfulness. I have never seen him like this before. Once again, we go for a long walk. I ask him if he is not sometimes tempted to abandon his brushes in favor of his pen. He bursts out laughing. A few seconds later:

"No, painters have written too much already. They should keep quiet. And, as you know, words reject me.

"The pity of it is that words are so important. But words aren't life.

"People talk to attack, or to defend themselves. But a person who refuses to talk . . .

"A painting is such a mystery . . . It's a sudden illumination. You can't explain it.

"Everyone tries to be smart. To be a smart-ass.

"People's lives are a complete illusion. But woe to anyone who becomes aware of it.

"It is extremely difficult not to cheat.

"No, it's not easy. The outside world is constantly trying to destroy you.

"What makes a painting fascinating is its sincerity. Sincerity is such a rare thing. Most people don't dare to be sincere.

"Life is nothing but being stabbed, knifed. We are the wound."

I ask him the reason for his despair.

"Because it's an adventure out of all proportion. You have to devote all your strength to it and it's never enough."

He talks several times about the solitude of the artist. He lived in Paris for thirty-five years but only ever had one friend, Beckett, and even they did not meet very frequently.

"If you're not on the same wavelength as all the others, you can go to hell.

"It's crazy how many lost souls there are. And they are the best.

"No, I never considered giving up painting and looking for a job."

He has been destitute, or at least extremely poor, all his life. Often, he has only just managed to survive.

"Sometimes, when you least expect it, life proves to be malleable.

"When you resign yourself to this compulsion, it is as though it influences your circumstances and has the power to make the impossible possible. Sometimes truly miraculous things happen. Meeting Beckett was a truly miraculous stroke of luck.

"It is true that other people can help you, and to lasting effect.

"If I hadn't had Beckett in 1940, I'm not so sure I could have stood it. I am really not sure."

He talks about their relationship and explains to me how Beckett had demonstrated from the start that he had vision.

"At that time, he was driven by an extremely aggressive and fiery Irish spirit. That has lessened as time has gone on."

I remark that the latest photographs of Beckett show his face losing the ironic humor that permeated his features when he was younger.

"Yes," he agrees, "he is tending to lose all individuality."

After a long pause:

"I don't know anywhere in modern art any more faithful or more impressive picture of contemporary humanity than the one he offers us in *The Unnamable*."

We return to the subject of painting.

"No, I have never painted at night. Colors change under electric light. You can't feel the color any more.

"X . . . There was one thing he didn't know, and that was that, in a sense, the thing is impossible. Where that's concerned, there are two camps: there are those who recognize this drama and there are the others. The two are worlds apart.

"People like that want somebody like Kandinsky or Mondrian to be right, and to rule out all other possibilities.

"Fear has played a great part in my life. It can be illuminating. Fear is connected with painting, it comes from the invisible."

He tells me about Nicolas de Staël's two visits to him.

In the morning he can sit for three hours on end meditating, concentrating, but never thinking about his current painting.

"So many things go through your mind."

He has read a few pages of my *Journal*. They reminded him of a statue of Sainte-Beuve which stands, if I understand him correctly, in the Jardin du Luxembourg, and which bears on its base the almost indecipherable inscription: "The truth, nothing but the truth."

"I have been to look at that statue several times, just to drink in those few words.

"It's a never-ending battle between truth and falsehood."

He tells me how, perhaps just before the war, he was taking part in a group exhibition and was surprised one day, on arriving at the gallery, to find a man standing in front of one of his paintings holding forth on it to a crowd gathered around him. Bram stopped to listen without revealing his identity. Years later, a stranger accosted him in the street and Bram immediately recognized the man who had gone to such lengths to communicate his enthusiasm about that painting to the other visitors at the exhibition. They introduced themselves. It was the sculptor Vitullo.

"Like me, he had a long fight against poverty. And at the end of his life, a retrospective was organized in the area he came from. But they were just exploiting him for political ends. I don't know exactly what happened, but they abused his trust and—quite unwittingly—he got mixed up in an affair which left him utterly discredited and in despair. He died two months later."

November 2, 1970

He has always wanted to distance himself from the world of words, from explanations that explain nothing. He speaks of a fragile history. Of the need to preserve the mystery of painting.

"They use words like weapons.

"Most of them are looking for possession. They don't realize that possession is impossible.

"You have to be devoid of all resources. You have to abandon yourself. To trust to a profound oblivion.

"People fear the impossible.

"I am well aware that a painting must inevitably be a bizarre, incomprehensible thing.

"I start off on the canvas and, little by little, it imposes its own solution. But that solution is not easy to find.

"A painting is not a battle against other people, but against oneself." (In an interview, he notes that he has never made a polemical painting.)

"Painting, an oeuvre, is not such a big deal, it's so unimportant. But that's precisely what makes it interesting.

"It takes such energy to paint."

We look at his last two paintings. A savage power and vehemence. Something visceral. Elementary.

"I don't know if I've got close enough to what I was really trying to achieve. But at least I've tried, I've made the attempt. I've done what I could. I've gone as far as my powers permitted."

And I am suddenly reminded of what Beckett noted in his first text:

> Impossible to apply reason to what is unique. [. . .]
> Impossible to create order in what is elemental.[13]

November 1, 1971

Bram, still totally focused on the inexpressible. He often shakes with silent laughter when he realizes what he has just said. Sometimes, he even seems taken aback. And his strange way of making the invisible, in a few words, suddenly almost visible, palpable.

We look at his most recent gouaches. So different from all those he's painted before. And he is seventy-six years old. The flexibility of mind that must lie behind them. And the abundant vitality that informs their shapes and colors. A feeling of amplitude and freedom. Like so many great painters of the past, it is now that he is producing his greatest works. The spirit has achieved transparency; it is able now to efface itself and to offer free passage to whatever passes through it and organizes itself on the canvas. Gouaches like these are like X-ray images of the state to which he has acceded. I am caused violently to evoke in my mind all the years of suffering, of unrelenting effort and of failure, which were required for the spirit to attain such flexibility, such freedom and abandon.

"If these gouaches live at all, it is because they are true, they derive from life. They are born of the unknown—and not of habit, or know-how, or intention, or of some recipe."

Echoing what I have just told him about my work:

"There comes a time when serious work is no longer an effort. When demanding work of that kind no longer tires you.

"You just have to give back what you have received.

"Sometimes, you work, you do your best, but there is no reward. The thing escapes you, you can't get inside it.

"Too many artists play it safe and keep within the bounds of the possible.

"Above all, never affirm.

"However terrible it is, the thing never involves any sadness.

"You have to succeed in severing yourself from this unceasing torrent of words.

"It's important to see that my paintings are ultimately stimulating. They are not at all the kind of thing that inspires despair."

We talk about Beckett and his writings about Bram.

"He managed to find words which broke with that kind of writing and which were compatible with my attempt to go beyond conventional forms. He told me he wanted to 'strip away all the humbug.'"

We continue for some time to talk about Beckett. I express my admiration for his pared-down style, uncontaminated by intellectualism or rhetoric.

"That's right, he has managed to live without his head."

(And I recall this passage taken from the only interview that, so far as I know, Beckett has ever granted a French newspaper:

—*I never read philosophy.*

—Why not?

—*I don't understand it.*

[. . .]

—Why did you write your books?

—*I don't know. I'm not an intellectual. I just feel things. I invented* Molloy *and the rest on the day I understood how stupid I'd been. I began then to write down the things I feel.*)[14]

A moment later Bram adds:

"I think that's what I've tried to produce too. Something devoid of artifice."

April 3, 1972

"You have to sever yourself from this world, this life we lead.

"You have to find the strength to break the spell.

"Painting is getting in touch with the truth. It's a matter of summoning up the vision I need.

"You are in an area where knowledge fails. Where you have to advance in ignorance, not even knowing where you are going.

"You have to do what only you can do.

"An oeuvre is like a chain: you manufacture it link by link.

"When you go a long way away, you necessarily distance yourself from other people. But in the intervals between work, you do to some extent rejoin the human world.

"I like walking. Walking is always a pleasure.

"Those who love the thing are not free. It's people who don't love it who can afford to do what they like.

"The real horror is mass production. Painting when there is no compulsion to do so.

"Pictures like that are all unpunished crimes.

"Look at the young people in the universities . . . The whole tenor of the times drives people to seek to control."

We talk about Artaud:

"He has fallen apart. And you can understand how that can happen to a person. He is so fragile. Beckett's different: he has managed to contain his drive towards madness.

"Nobody listens to you. They are all busy pursuing their own little track, never looking left or right. So it's just hard luck for anyone who's trying to achieve a global vision."

Every time I see him, what strikes me is his refusal to make conversation, his aversion to words. So our meetings are dominated by immense stretches of silence. Then I ask a question and the response springs from his lips, brief and to the point. Sometimes it appears to take even him by surprise and he seems, like me, to be left groping to understand its meaning. At times, too, his reply remains in suspense, either because he has become lost in his thoughts or, more rarely, because he fails to find the word he's looking for. But I have never once heard him utter anything that was false, arguable, inadequate, or even approximate.

At each of our meetings he insists that the artist must be without knowledge, without power, without will. That he must not intervene, not control, not seek to produce, but rather allow himself to be borne along by whatever comes to him and demands to come into the world.

And so it is that he is supposed to make some lithographs and ink drawings for a collection of Hölderlin poems[15] and a Blanchot story,[16] but is currently unable to do it and has for some months been waiting. He is determined above all not to force things. I can't help thinking that, with over half a century of painting behind him and with his mastery of his craft, he would find it quite easy to produce rapidly what is expected—even under pressure to meet deadlines imposed on him from outside—if he did not impose this implacable demand on himself.

I have also dried up at the moment and confess to him how difficult I find it.

"When you are working, you are so far away and so absorbed, it's inevitable that you fall into a vacuum when you stop.

"Every time I finish a painting, I always have to wait to get my strength back before I can begin another."

May, 1972

Louvre Dialogues[17] has just been published. Describing his visit to the Louvre with Bram, Pierre Schneider notes:

> Van Velde feels committed only from the point at which painting becomes impossible, when its very absurdity permits him to express the absurdity of the human condition.

And later:

> Throughout our tour, Van Velde's eye will reveal the Achilles heel, the almost imperceptible flaw which undermines the entire edifice and through the breach gives a glimpse of a more essential truth underlying the apparent coherence.

And from Bram I should like to record these few words:

"I am in a thousand pieces. Painting somehow makes me whole.

"Painting lives only through the slide towards the unknown in oneself.

"It's not easy to see. It even requires a degree of courage and you haven't always got it.

"The world of architecture—and of works conceived for architecture—tends towards beauty. True painting tends towards ugliness and panic."

And, contemplating the painting of a particular period:

"If you look at art seriously, it somehow isn't even serious. It's a funny story that makes you weep. Or vice versa."

His silences. Their density. The effervescence that suffuses them. The feeling of strangeness that they generate. And what excites and impresses me is to feel the invisible so intensely present in him, this thing that possesses him and in which he can at any moment submerge himself, his eyes staring and absent.

"My pictures suggest things but never state them. They don't attempt to persuade or to prove anything.

"My pictures are also an annihilation.

"When I paint, I don't know what I'm doing or where I'm going. I have to look for a way out. I go on working until I don't have to do anymore.

"Creating a painting is a matter of ensuring that all its parts achieve unity. Though it's a precarious, fragile unity.

"Failure is more common than success. In painting as in life.

"You have to allow yourself to be controlled.

"Something is trying to come into the world. But I don't know what it is. I never start by knowing. It's impossible to know. Truth is not knowledge.

"Words are nothing. They're just noises. You have to distrust them deeply. When I approach a canvas, I encounter silence.

"This mechanical world is asphyxiating us. Painting is life.

"Life is not in the visible.

"The canvas allows me to make the invisible visible."

We go over to the garage he uses as a studio. Four gouaches are pinned to boards leaning against the wall. They represent his output over several weeks, yet they look as if they were painted in great haste. Every movement of the brush is visible.

The colors are mixed, heavy, primitive. But sometimes there are delicate areas of transparency. A great lightness.

I remark that he never uses pure colors.

"That's how it is. The colors are imposed on me. If they were pure, it wouldn't be true."

He alludes in passing to what Beckett has written. I find this passage in a notebook:

> The situation is that of him who is helpless, cannot act, in the event cannot paint, since he is obliged to paint. The act is of him who, helpless, unable to act, acts, in the event paints, since he is obliged to paint.[18]

"A painting is a kind of miracle."

I talk about the surprising structure of his works, always obvious although difficult to grasp.

"I need to go towards the illogical. This world we live in destroys us. It is always governed by the same laws. You have to create images that don't belong to it. That are totally different from those it presents us."

I talk again about the structure of his works, open and as if in perpetual movement.

"Of course. Life never stands still.

"The greatest moment is when you realize that the painting you've just finished is nothing. When you manage to detach yourself from it.

"Mondrian? . . . The Constructivists? . . . They had certainties. They wanted a stable basis to work on, but I'm afraid that that was enormous arrogance on their part. Nothing is stable and no certainties are possible."

We return to the tree under which he sits and meditates for hours on end.

"I sit here doing nothing. But I am hard at work.

"The most difficult time is when you're doing nothing. When you haven't the strength to work.

"Painting is a bit like witchcraft.

"What the eye can see won't get us very far. And what it can see is so limited, so restricted. But a gouache or an oil painting can be seen at a glance, can take in a whole world at a single glance.

"I can't use words. Sometimes, of course, they are useful to a degree. But they can't express the essentials."

In fact, he manages to talk without sentences. And yet, you understand exactly what he wants to say, even though there is never any line of argument or train of thought. Nothing but the fact, the unadorned statement, the sudden illumination passing through it.

August 29, 1972

"Yes, somehow, we are all the same."

He's reading Schopenhauer these days.

"There's a lot of truth in it. At times it's even quite close to Beckett. But of course at other times you disagree."

I ask him if he has ever experienced ennui.

"Not really. I have always been sustained by what I was going to do."

For the last ten years he has been taking sleeping pills at bedtime:

"You have to stop your head going round at night."

We go out to sit under a tree in the garden:

"This is where I work hardest.

"Art isn't working. It's not doing something. It's something else entirely."

He says how much he admires Matisse, although he's never tried to meet him. At one time, in Paris, he visited a gallery several times to look at *The Piano Lesson,* a painting he especially likes. He knew Matisse's daughter, who once gave him an old coat of her father's. And, chortling, he tells me how much he enjoyed wearing that coat, even though it didn't suit him at all. And suddenly, without transition, with an expression of stunning gravity:

"People who have never experienced destitution can't understand anything."

Just recently, he happened to meet a woman who talked to him about his painting as if she understood it. He confesses that he is always amazed when anyone speaks kindly to him.

"So often people try to destroy you."

In response to a confidence on my part:

"There is very little one can do for other people.

"It is very difficult to help others without betraying them."

He spent four years in Majorca and produced six paintings there. I remark on his low productivity during those years.

"No, no, I was quite satisfied."

We go over to the garage to see the two large gouaches he has just finished.

"They are terrible, aren't they?" And he shakes with silent, embarrassed laughter. Then, gravely:

"One is so alone.

"I think there is a degree of primitivism in what I do.

"You have to see without illusions. Without trying to protect yourself.

"You can't know anything. Knowledge is no use.

"There is only the present. A painting is an instant of time that has escaped oblivion.

"I feel myself tied to life. To the immensity and complexity of life. Each painting is an impulse towards life.

"You have to keep as low as you can."

(Beckett confided to Maurice Nadeau[19] one day: "I can't write. I'm not low enough.")

"Painters who get a taste of success get so diverted from life."

I go on studying the gouaches. What tragedy! But also what vitality and abundance! A kind of magma in which a structure can be discerned that is difficult to grasp, and where life is supposed to be captured in its essence. I feel that they depict all the conditions in which the spirit stagnates, or which it traverses in its quest for unity, all its vicissitudes and confrontations, and the extremes between which the web of our condition hangs taut: fragility and force, the inexhaustible questioning and quietness, ephemerality and permanence, a serene tension and the exercise of a most flexible freedom, fragmentation and the imminence of unity, equilibrium under threat and a kind of sovereign amplitude. A disaster. An exultation. And each state is constantly mutating and becoming its opposite. Or, to be more precise, one's reading oscillates between one state and the other, until the spirit is convulsively inundated by the overspill of these harsh and delicate colors. I think back over what Bram has just said and see that, faced with a vision so tragic yet so true to reality, the idea of success must appear not only derisory but actually improper.

"Life is a struggle. So is painting.

"A painting must preserve its mystery. The painter is the guardian of that mystery.

"I have no roof, no refuge."

We talk about Beckett.

"He never cheats. He has the strength to be himself whatever happens. He's a truly exceptional person.

"He's not like me. He uses words. Words are powerful. I haven't even had that."

I quote a passage I came across in a brief text by Beckett, published long ago in an issue of the *Lettres Nouvelles*: "The artist who stakes his being is from nowhere, has no kith."[20]

My remark prefaced in this way, I tell him that I find him very like Beckett.

"Oh no . . . He is very different from me. He's an exceptional person. A kind of archangel. He really comes from on high, whereas I come from below, from the cave. He is an absolutely extraordinary person."

And after a long pause:

"So mysterious . . ."

He goes on to tell me how once, when he was living in Paris, Beckett came to visit him for the first time in a new studio. In fact, it was an old loft that Bram had fixed up.

Coming in, Beckett grabbed hold of a stick that was lying around and banged against the rafters with it, as if to test their solidity and make sure that the roof wasn't about to collapse. Then he inspected the pictures. Bram was going through a period of enormous concentration, he had been working desperately hard and for once wasn't too unhappy with the results. So he told Beckett that he was almost satisfied.

Beckett, expressionlessly:

"There's really no reason to be."

Totally thrown by this response, Bram retreated to a corner of the studio, where he sat down at the table and began to eat to cover his confusion. Meanwhile, Beckett stood motionless in the middle of the loft, fixing him with his eagle eye.

October 29, 1972

Invited by some new friends to have lunch with Madeleine and Bram. Another couple were also there, whom we have also only recently met. It was the first time that I had seen Bram out of his own setting, among other people. But of course he was no different. The same long silences. The same startled, unhappy expression in those eyes, which suddenly, without transition, assail you with an unblinking stare of intimidating intensity.

After the meal, he talked freely and with enthusiasm, but I was tense and ill at ease and had to make my own contribution to the conversation, so that I was never able to stand back as I usually do in the course of an exchange to memorize what has just been said. So I have forgotten most of what Bram told us. I have been able to recall these few fragments, however:

"I am a watered-down being."

And, although I can't guarantee that these were his exact words:

"If it weren't for all this water, I would be a stone.

"I am a walker. When I'm not working, I have to walk. I walk so that I can go on working.

"The eye works independently of you. You live by the eye.

"'He imprisons himself, but he escapes from his prison.' Duthuit[21] wrote that somewhere. That's a good description of what happens. He studied my work for years before talking about it.

"Beckett? There is nobody more silent. From time to time he used to let slip a few words. But they were not encouraging."

He talks about artists who dodge life and play a role. Repeats several times that he can't trust words, that those he uses do not represent him. Goes so far as to claim that what he says is not true, so untrue, insufficient, inadequate, and disproportionate do words seem in relation to the significance with which he burdens them.

He speaks again of the distress to which the artist is prey and maintains that every life, every work, represents nothing but failure. Mireille rebels against this assertion and he becomes panic-stricken. I intervene to suggest that distress cannot be unbroken, that he must have known moments when he was filled with comparative happiness and fulfillment.

"When a canvas is 'flat' (when it is finished, when all the elements are in equilibrium and the struggle is over, when he finds that he can see the canvas as a painting), I am jubilant. There really is a moment of jubilation."

And, as he tells us about it, his open palms raised on either side of his face, his eyes shine intensely blue.

"But the vision only lasts for a moment, and then there is the backlash." (And I can't help thinking of Rilke: "For glory lasts only a moment, and we have never seen anything that is longer than misery.")[22]

We refer to his total submission to the compulsion that possesses him and which I find quite logically rules out any regard for social status. How could any ambition of that kind be reconciled with the need to renounce the self (by which I mean the particular individual ego with all its conditioning, its limitations, its need to possess and control, etc.), *to keep as low as possible*, to go with the current, to remain in distress, to sacrifice one's own identity to life? I go on to try to explain how, in my view, the artistic process is inconceivable without rigorous ethical standards. But he says nothing, we get bogged down, and once again I am furious at the difficulty of expressing what I want to say, even though I am literally suffocating with the obvious truth of it.

Marie-Madeleine expresses astonishment that he never repeats himself, that his painting continues to change.

"It's because it's linked to life. I am always on the move, and it's always new, always different. That's also why I have produced so little."

I spur him on to talk about his life in Paris and the years of destitution he experienced. But once again I am forced to accept that for him the past is a dead letter: he has completely forgotten; he can tell us nothing about it.

I ask him what he meant when he said that "painting is proceeding towards destruction." As always when I ask for explanations, he looks away panic-stricken and silence sets in, grows longer, turns into a kind of malaise, and I sense that he is lost. We come to his rescue, try to sketch a possible response.

"Yes, the destruction of all the screens, of every obstacle to vision.

"Van Gogh? . . . He was a beacon. Not like me. I just feel my way in the dark. But I am good at feeling my way."

I am secretly amazed at this and note his immediate confusion, for it is the first time that I have ever heard him say anything even hinting at self-satisfaction.

"What is so wonderful is that all that (painting, an oeuvre, the role of the artist . . .) is so pointless and yet so necessary."

When he speaks, this mixture of enthusiasm and constraint. His gentleness. An undeniable innocence and candor. Also his meticulous precision and, sometimes, when he fears that the person to whom he is speaking doesn't agree with him, and he is on the verge of panic, something approaching supplication.

And an innocuous little incident comes back to me. It was insignificant, really, but it struck me at the time.

It was the first time I ever visited Bram in Geneva. We had been out walking and were returning by car when he caught sight of a horse in a field.

Turning to me, he kept repeating over and over again, "Horse . . . horse . . . horse . . . "—pointing at it with all the eagerness of an excited child.

October 30, 1972

I saw him again this morning. He was gloomy and discontented after a sleepless night and I found it hard to make contact. He was angry with himself for "talking too much" and I suspect that he was tormented with persistent remorse about that "I am good at feeling my way."

"You come across so many dramas. That is what weighs you down and often paralyzes you.

"Whenever people talk about painting, they're immediately wide of the mark.

"What I have done is only a feeble attempt."

Once again, I discuss the painting[23] at the Stedelijk Museum in Amsterdam with him. It exudes such a feeling of success, of fulfillment, you feel every element is so perfectly integrated, that the slightest change would upset the whole difficult equilibrium of the composition. I ask him how many such obviously successful paintings he thinks he has made.

"Perhaps ten. Not more. (Transcribing these notes, I discover that I asked him the same question four years earlier and got the same reply.) In the others, I got somewhere near what I was trying to achieve, but I never quite made it. It's not so easy to achieve.

"No, I don't draw. In a drawing, you always know more or less where you're going. It's not an adventure. I need that leap into the unknown."

I ask him if he has read the oriental "philosophers." He doesn't know, can't remember.

"You just have to look inside yourself. It's all there.

"I read books less and less. But I do flip through the newspapers. All those events, crises, dramas, convulsions . . . Literature pales by comparison.

"Even as a child, I wanted to paint. As far back as I can remember."

And he describes the unforgettable excitement he felt when, at the age of five or six, he was given a box of crayons and began right away to color with them. On my last visit, I had given him Matisse's *Ecrits et propos sur l'art*, and now we talk about him.

"He says somewhere that one day he felt like going for a walk but couldn't because he had to work. But the reason was that he found satisfaction in it. It's different for me. I am often driven. Really, I no longer have anything but the quest. I don't even have work to keep me going."

We look at the lithographs he has made to accompany Hölderlin's poems and Maurice Blanchot's story. I find them extremely beautiful.

"No, it's not the real thing yet. They just helped me wait. Not to give way to fatigue."

Picasso died a few weeks before this meeting. I bring up his name and we talk about him at length. To begin with, I observe that Bram has produced fewer paintings in his entire life than Picasso in his final year, even though he was over ninety by that time.

"Admittedly he was exceptionally creative and inventive. But he was a stranger to doubt. He never felt his way, and he was unconscious of the drama. All his life, he was spurred on by the need for more: more pictures, more money, and you could almost say more women . . . (and I suddenly recall what Beckett wrote in his study of Proust: "The artistic tendency is not expansive, but a contraction. And art is the apotheosis of solitude.")[24] The most difficult thing is to do nothing. Just look around you and see how people rush around and fuss and struggle. You'd think it was the most difficult thing in the world just to do nothing. They say he was still working the day before he died. Isn't that crazy? If something had happened, what did he have to add? And look how people admire worldly success and wealth . . . That sort of success was a constant crutch to him. But when you're looking for life, you don't need a crutch. Just to be alone, doubting and questioning."

After a long pause:

"I have never had anything to lean on, never any certainty. Often, I have been on the verge of being destroyed.

"You have to go where you are led.

"I have remained in touch with life. I have never mass-produced. Never lied.

"It's a rare artist who is ready to do only what life permits."

At the end of this meeting, I would like to add that I have never once detected in what he says, or in his attitude towards me, any hint of his trying to take advantage of his age, experience, or oeuvre to impose his opinions on me, to force me to agree with him or—worse still—to assume any right to feel superior. Nor has he ever spoken to me in a tone of peremptory assurance, with that trenchant authority suggesting that any objection or challenge will be met by a bad-tempered rejoinder or annoyed silence.

Well so what, you may say, that's nothing out of the ordinary; it's what you have every right to expect. Of course. But perhaps it's not so very common as to be unworthy of mention. (A right, I said. In accordance with the fundamental law that tells us that the only way to discover yourself is through detachment and self-effacement, through a dissolution of self, in journeying towards anonymity, or in taking care to free oneself of all need for self affirmation and control.)

June 11, 1973

When I arrive these days I have the feeling he is pleased to see me. Our talk is increasingly friendly, easier, more familiar in tone. And this evening I am quite moved when I think back to my first meeting with him. To those moments of embarrassment, which were amongst the worst I have ever experienced. I was impatient to engage in a dialogue and I overwhelmed him with incautious and incoherent questions. They fell flat, and the silence grew deeper and deeper, becoming more unbearable by the second, until I got so embarrassed that I began to wonder whether I shouldn't just go away.

"A painting is an instant of vision.

"I can never trust to words."

And he explains to me how much more appropriate he finds music and painting than words to put us in touch with the inexpressible. He has recently seen a film with a score taken from Mahler.[25]

"Just a few notes. And the horror of real life is instantly banished, leaving the spirit free. Suddenly it's a different world.

"Painting is a vital necessity.

"You have to create an image that's never been seen before.

"I have never been able to understand artists who work to a set timetable, like civil servants.

"You have to reveal the invisible."

Standing in the garage, we inspect his most recent work. I am particularly struck by one gouache. A structure imposes itself, apparently obvious, and the eye begins to run down the painting from top to bottom. Then, suddenly, you realize that there is a different way to read it. So you abandon the first and switch to the second. But already, there's a third possibility . . . So you are borne along, then soon lost, with nothing to lean on—to borrow his expression—immersed in the color, in these currents of energy, these tensions, these transparencies, this kind of profusion that exudes a feeling of streaming vitality—as if life had been seized at its very source.

I talk to Bram about this thwarted reading and the ingeniously labyrinthine structure he has contrived.

"That's what is so difficult to sustain to the end. It's exhausting."

He recalls something Duthuit once wrote about a painting of his, in which he referred to "a drowned city alight with captive suns."

"It's these moments (indicating the gouaches) that sometimes keep you going, help you to carry on.

"There is no knowledge."

I ask him about the retrospective due to be held in December at the Fondation Maeght. As I have often noticed before, his work is the only thing of fundamental concern to him. He seems to regard an exhibition as marginal. He can't get interested in it—I think because he doesn't feel free to let go of his preoccupations. So when an exhibition is being organized, he never knows when it is, which paintings are to be selected, or if there is to be a catalogue.

"I put myself entirely in Jacques Putman's hands."

He tells me about his fear, his dread of starting work at the beginning of the afternoon. He is preparing himself but at the same time postponing the moment when he will have to sit down and face his canvas.

"But there comes a moment when I can't not do it any more.

"Painting often scares me. It takes such energy.

"Painting has to struggle to beat back this world, which cannot but assassinate the invisible.

"I only reveal what exists.

"When I can't work, I don't abandon it. I prepare myself to welcome what awaits me."

His gouaches give you the feeling of concealing some kind of inevitability. Hence their intensity. And although they are obviously finished, clearly brought to maximum fulfillment, they remain in movement. The life that the painter has struggled to amass and compress onto these surfaces has not been mutilated, or reduced to any rigid scheme that would merely serve as its shell. It is there, in its entirety. And it circulates, flowing, free, savage, irrepressible, ungraspable, producing doubt, surrender, bewilderment, passion, weariness, and wonder. And each gouache entails a new struggle, new risks, a new invention, new colors, a dangerous and unstable new equilibrium. And each time there is the same disappointment, the same feeling of failure, of being yoked to a task that is utterly vain, exhausting, and impossible. And each failure engenders the same compulsion to try again, the same illusion of certainty that the next attempt will allow him to approach a little closer to the unapproachable. And each time, there is the same impatience, the same urgency, the same haste.

Hence these gouaches: vehement, harsh, strained yet serene, light and yet powerful, intense, alien, and convincing, reflecting that totality of life of which they are the expression.

He points out his most recent gouache:

"Perhaps in that there is a certain spiritual happiness."

And he laughs the silent, embarrassed laugh that is so typical of the man.

Bram and his candor. His capacity for wonder and his child-like reactions. His vulnerability. Always tense, fearful, needing to smile or laugh to escape his embarrassment, or to defend himself against your eyes.

Madeleine has told us that in 1938 he spent a month in prison in Bayonne for failing to renew his residence papers. This period in prison was a traumatic experience and he bore the scars for many years. Even now, he still finds it difficult to go through customs and has actually foregone travel in order to avoid border crossings.

During those thirty days of imprisonment, he scribbled a few drawings on envelopes and whatever bits of paper he managed to obtain. Jacques Putman offers to put together a little book of these drawings and suggests that, if Bram would agree to talk to me about what the experience meant to him and about its sequels, what he told me could be used as a text to accompany the drawings.[26] But his response is brusque:

"Yes, I suppose so, but it was so little compared with what other people have been through. Irritations and dramas are important and necessary. You have to learn not to avoid them."

(I am aware that, written down like this, these phrases of Bram's lose their vitality and impact. I suppose their initial power to shock and illuminate derives less from what Bram says than from the way he says it. He speaks with such gravity, with a capacity for wonder that communicates his pleasure in discovery, and with a neutral intensity that seems, as it were, to place his words outside of time, so that you really feel what he is expressing. He charges the words he uses with such singular density that they evoke in you something equivalent to what they convey. When Bram says, for example, "You experience some funny things in your life," you are seized by the self-evident truth of the assertion. You are suddenly surprised by an acute awareness of the peculiarity of the inner voice that murmurs within you, and of all that the mental process throws up and liberates from time to time.)

In some notes on my reading, I find this interview that a Swiss newspaper requested from Beckett after he was awarded the Nobel Prize. I will surrender to the urge to transcribe it here:

> We so often find ourselves in states that have no connection with the "real" world . . . through his work, Samuel Beckett helps us to recapture them. A large proportion of our life is mechanical, we are afraid of discovering what is really going on, of exploring our fragility, and we cannot find the words to formulate our fear. Beckett expresses it so accurately that our recognition makes us stronger. He is free, he does not allow himself to be led by preconceptions. He advances alone, in search of that little-known being that lies at the heart of ourselves.[27]

And from another interview, on the occasion of his retrospective at the Musée d'Art Moderne, I would like to record these few words, since I cannot bear to think of them perishing together with the paper on which they were printed.

"To paint is to be engulfed, to take the plunge.

"The more lost you are, the more you are driven downwards towards the root of things, into the depths.

"I have had no assistance from the intellect. I may be sensitive to many things but nothing can help me. Nothing but the necessity of the image.

"The drama overwhelms you.

"There's something inside me trying to get out, something that can't not exist.

"A picture is an effort to get at the source, an inquiry into the mystery of life undertaken with one's entire being.

"The work consumes me.

"The painter is also blind, but he needs to see."[28]

July 31, 1973

. . . in the immovable masses of a being shut away and shut off and turned inward for ever, pathless, airless, cyclopean, lit with flares and torches, colored with the colors of the spectrum of blackness.

An endless unveiling, veil behind veil, plane after plane of imperfect transparencies, light and space themselves veils, an unveiling towards the unveilable, the nothing, the thing again. And burial in the unique, in a place of impenetrable nearness, cell painted on the stone of cell, art of confinement.

These lines, taken from "La peinture des Van Velde,"[29] were written by Beckett in 1948. Although Bram's way of painting has not changed radically since then, it seems to me that we could now no longer have recourse to the term "confinement" to describe it. What strikes me in the oils and gouaches of these last few years is their liberty, their ease (and all the implications this word calls up when you consider the immense labor he has to perform on himself in order to arrive at what he depicts—this ease of movement within himself in a substance almost at rest and on the way to becoming homogeneous), and the peaceful and impetuous life that runs through them and confers a majestic amplitude on them. The flame leaps and brightens, the eye is laid bare, the adventure becomes ever more intense, and so—like some of the great artists of the past—he has painted with the most freedom and power in the evening of his life. We talk about our journey, about a traffic accident. I can feel Bram tensing up and I note his unease. We agree with Madeleine that it would be better to change the subject. Bram nods. Then, his words punctuated by that embarrassed laugh of his, he tells us how once, at the barber's, a man started to describe a serious accident that he had witnessed. Bram couldn't stand it and had to rush away, pursued by the astonished stares of the other customers. Noting the vivacity with which he recounts this anecdote, I ask him if it happened on his last visit to the barber:

"No, no . . . It was in Holland . . . In 1922 . . .

"The artist has nothing but enemies. The struggle goes on every second and on every front.

"When you can't work, you feel excluded and it hurts. But when the work's going well, you feel as if you're floating."

He's been working for weeks on a gouache that won't come out right and he prefers not to show it to me.

"When the work isn't going well, it's not liberating at all. It's more like a massacre.

"You have to give it your all and it's exhausting.

"No, I have never had children. It just happened like that. It wasn't a deliberate decision."

Some years ago, he went to New York (where he met a number of artists including Willem de Kooning and Barnett Newman). We talk about the trip:

"It's like a film you see . . . But nothing comes of it."

In the afternoon, we go for a walk in the cornfields. We pause without speaking to watch the combine-harvesters, then walk on. After a lengthy silence, he talks about people who live contentedly, at peace with themselves, apparently without questioning their lot.

"The misery begins when you lose that innocence. Artists are so far away from it, they can't but be unhappy.

"Perhaps artists suffer from a lack of being. They use their work to fill the vacuum. To try to be. But they know perfectly well that they are not living, they are not part of life.

"Once, in Paris, I was in a café. In one of those glassed-in cafés that project onto the pavement. There was a man sitting there, not looking out into the street like all the other customers, but facing inwards towards them. The look in his eyes was unforgettable. You see, he was feeding on all those faces. A few days later, I found out it was Antonin Artaud."

We talk about Artaud's letters, which he has just been reading.

"His spirit burned. Only people who are familiar with suffering have anything to say."

I talk to him about Beckett's eyes.

"Yes, they are frightening, sometimes. You see such lucidity in them.

"Beckett shows us what is."

I tell him that I have had to dig up something I'd written and almost forgotten about, and that I was extremely disappointed to find it was so strongly influenced by Beckett.

"It doesn't matter. It's not important. You have to have antecedents. Every artist has been through it.

"Beckett . . . he's a real man. When you've known someone like him, so many other people seem like mere robots by comparison. Or like bad actors pretending to be ordinary people.

"Rilke? . . . Yes, he was an outsider. He never had a role.

"You have to be able to take risks. To do without defenses, either against the outside world or against your inner self.

"Baudelaire? . . . He invented the naked human spirit.

"His great merit was that he managed to avoid embellishment.

"Picasso's curse was never being able to do nothing.

"If there weren't all this phoniness around, our efforts to achieve the truth wouldn't be needed or justified.

"The truth is upsetting and frightening, so the world is determined to stifle it.

"Falsity is given every encouragement and it's a miracle if truth survives at all.

"If there were only the truth, we shouldn't be aware of it.

"When I see paintings I made in the past, like in Brussels recently, they are me and at the same time completely alien and nothing to do with me.

"There is something very primitive in what I do.

"No, I have never had to impose a disciplined way of life on myself. I existed to paint and there was never any room for anything else.

"You have to obliterate the world with what you make.

"Sometimes, you no longer have the strength to do what is true. And you feel that you could quite well become entirely bankrupt.

"Basically, all this is never anything but a huge respect for life."

When we are preparing to leave, he tells us again that he can't bear to stay there any longer, in this setting and this town. He simply must have a change of scene. In November they will be leaving Geneva.

"Sometimes, I have hung on somewhere for a while, but it was never permanent. I am a man from nowhere."

We leave. And while, as after every meeting, my brain is working feverishly to recapture every word he said, while I am tortured by the fear of forgetting a particular remark and my mind keeps going over and over his words until they are safely transcribed, I realize that—although he has often talked to me about his ardent study of life—he has never once talked about death or the fear of death, or about his great age, which has allowed him to accede to such youthfulness.

One summer day in 1938, accompanied by Marthe Arnaud, Bram was walking along a path, not far from Bayonne. On the other side of the Pyrenees, war was raging. The police approached them. They asked for their papers, since they'd been conversing in German. Bram hadn't renewed his residency card. He was arrested on the spot, then incarcerated in the Bayonne prison. He was only there for four weeks, but those four weeks had changed him dramatically, had marked this extremely sensitive and impressionable man forever . . .

Yesterday, I wanted to take advantage of his relaxed mood to return to the subject. I came up against a categorical refusal:

"Such atrocities happen every day in Chile . . . How could I talk about those four weeks in prison?"

And after a long silence:

"Life is such a horror that one feels that anything can happen. If someone came around to shoot me tomorrow, I wouldn't even be surprised."

December 21-22, 1973

Retrospective at the Fondation Maeght. Bruno Roy presents us with the first copies of *Conversations with Bram van Velde,* which he has just published.[30]

At the end of November, we came with Rajak Ohanian, a photographer friend, to see Bram at Jacques's house in Grimaud, where he was planning to spend the next few months. We walked in the hills nearby, and the next day, in bright late autumn weather, spent some happy hours at La Chartreuse de la Vergne. Bram was glad to be away from Geneva and back in this house where he can enjoy the view down over the rolling hills every time he steps outside, and go for frequent drives in an area full of likely new discoveries. But, in the end, the visit seems to have been a disappointment. He couldn't get down to work, there were more and more rainy days, and he was often distressed at the extreme isolation of the house. He also found the total solitude oppressive.

I'd never had the chance to get to the Fondation, so it was a pleasure to visit it for the first time, thanks to the retrospective.

Once again, I discovered how one's perception of the paintings is influenced by the exhibition space. Here, in these spacious galleries, they have room to breathe. Studying them from a distance, I realize that their structure can be read much better that way and that they gain in amplitude. When I say so to Bram, he agrees:

"It's hardly surprising, given that this kind of painting is linked to space."

I introduce him to Truphémus, a painter friend who lives near me and whom I often visit in his studio. There was an immediate current of sympathy between the two and they talked for some time. Truphémus liked his paintings and was especially aware of the liberty they demonstrate, as well as the serenity, peace, and strength that emanates from them.

"You have to tell it all," adds Bram, "show it all."

I met his sister, Jacoba. Tall, good-looking, lively, youthful, with intensely blue eyes. She has produced Dutch translations of several works by Ionesco and Beckett.

For me, the best moment was seeing the film made about Bram several years ago by the painter Jean-Michel Meurice.[31] I was bowled over by the images. Bram walking in a Paris street amid falling snow. Or talking about his work, with his typical seriousness and concentration.

"Discouragement is an integral part of the adventure. Hope and despair are linked. Both are necessary parts of life.

"Everything you see or experience goes into the painting.

"To be able to speak, you have to have a role.

"You feel with so many people that they are just crippled.

"Before, painting was on the side of the positive, the feasible. I have had to go towards what is not feasible."

(I can't guarantee that this is a verbatim report. I was too moved to be able to memorize his words exactly.)

He also talked about his fear of painting. His fear of what he may discover. His fear of what painting reveals to him about himself.

Today, I went back to the gallery, both to study the paintings more closely and also—perhaps most especially—to see the film again.

Bram's face in close-up. Everything his eyes express or suggest. Sometimes—that extraordinary fixed, intense stare. And those words that spring from his lips, so very simple and yet so incisive. Never before have I felt his solitude, his anguish, his eccentricity, and the tragic nature of his adventure so strongly. Once again overwhelmed. Moved to tears.

The house is empty. We are both in the living room. It is late afternoon. A deep silence. I haven't seen Bram for the last three months. He is relaxed, and I feel that he will not mind talking, that he might even enjoy, for once, not exactly having a chat, but at least answering my questions.

However, we sit for a long time without speaking, silent, in meditative silence. But such is the feeling of intimacy that I feel that a current is passing between us, that we are in communication without needing to speak.

Then the dialogue begins, punctuated by very long pauses:

"Life is an invisible process of destruction.

"The artist is a person who has to attend to his spirit.

"You have to let it flow through you.

"I am a man without a tongue.

"You paint, but in fact everyone is blind.

"I have always had to be free. Not to have a role, or an occupation. My painting required it.

"I never know what's going to come out of me . . . That's why I live in this perpetual state of astonishment.

"Sometimes, I catch myself looking at myself like an actual stranger. As if I were an animal I'd never seen before. Of course, moments like that are always a bit dangerous. But fortunately they don't last long.

"I've lived a lot through my eyes.

"You have to be able to bring color to life.

"You are forced to keep to the impossible.

"When you need to begin a painting, you have to take a leap. A leap into the unknown. It's not easy."

The room is flooded with a golden, dying light. I look up. Facing me, on the wall, a painting with which I have long been familiar, but which remains alien to me. It's the only one in the room, and I think it is only there because Bram once gave it to his companion. Normally, once a painting is finished, he detaches himself from it and prefers to get rid of it so that it won't bar the way to the next one.

So this is a painting dating from some time ago, with a structure that is ample and well-defined, although impossible to describe, painted in dull, cloudy, grayish hues.

A painting that has always spurned my attempts to understand it. And, quite suddenly, I can see it. I can see the relationship between the tones, the harmony, the unity, the equilibrium that governs its various elements, and I savor the audacity that presided over its creation. The painting functions before my eyes and I feel its plenitude, its life, its secret intensity—and its surprising silence.

But perhaps it's no wonder that this painting should have bothered me so, even to the point of inspiring a degree of unease. After all, Bram's sole aim in his painting is to express his misery: the throes, the torment, and the inexhaustible suffering of one dedicated to the pursuit of the unattainable, the unimaginable, and the unnameable. Inevitably, therefore, this painting tends, in his own words, towards ugliness and panic. Hence the time it took for it to compel my recognition.

In the fading light, I tell Bram that I have just for the first time got inside this painting, experienced it, felt its life.

He is delighted. Then, a few minutes later:

"Looking at my paintings, you're facing life as it's seen. And that must always be a bit troubling.

"A painting is even more isolated, more dispossessed than a poem. It is constantly oriented towards an immense poverty.

"Painting is the guide to the blind man that is me.

"It may be one of the functions of a painting to amaze people. But to amaze them in a truthful way."

We go on to talk about the times, the conditions in which artists are forced to work and the difficulties he has encountered.

"People today are not so very different from the cavemen. It's still the same struggle to survive.

"This world is so terrible, so destructive. And it's so hard to beat it back and preserve a little of life.

"If I'd had words, I might perhaps have been able to escape from time to time. But without words . . .

"All these people who think they are good, generous, intelligent individuals, and who don't realize that they're dead.

"There is nothing worse than most religious people. It's crazy what people can do to obtain peace of mind.

"People are such cowards. But since cowardice is universal, nobody notices it anymore."

By now, night is falling and the shadows are growing deeper. The words seem to hang in the air, taking on extra intensity:

"We are surrounded by murderers.

"Alone against the world. I am the warrior of silence.

"The amazing thing is that, by keeping low, I have been able to go my own way.

"People who haven't known what it is to be destroyed haven't experienced life.

"Life is so dreadful, you feel that anything can happen."

Silence falls. I think about the gouache that he's been painting over the last few weeks and which I saw for the first time a few hours ago. Profusion, vitality, brimming with life—and yet the same feeling of tragedy as in all the others. I tell Bram what I am thinking and express my amazement:

"Well, of course," he replies. "You have to tell it all, show it all.

"A picture is almost nothing. Just a possibility which has arisen, and which will disappear just as quickly.

"It's odd . . . The thing sometimes comes just when you're beginning to lose hope of ever finding the solution.

"It's rare to be really satisfied with your work. To be able to feel that you've got somewhere near what you were hoping to achieve. But when it happens, it's never the result of an effort of will. The circumstances have to be exceptional . . . It's always a bit of a miracle . . .

"Of course, when you're painting, it is terribly difficult at times. But you have to be brave enough not to fear the worst.

"I have to gather the last of my strength."

Bram works in a garage where the conditions are far from ideal. Moreover, he can only work there in the summer. The rest of the year, he paints in a tiny room where, of course, he lacks space. And light. A few months ago his companion told me that he refuses to have a studio worthy of the name so as to remain faithful to his past life, to the destitution he has known, and not to join the ranks of the privileged, for whom everything is easy (at least, on the material level).

I tell him about the very fine portraits of him that Rajak Ohanian has made and which he has not yet seen.

"I don't like seeing photographs of myself. This wretched shell . . . And then, this mask is so often tragic it frightens me. I only like seeing paintings, because they are linked to life. They move. Photographs are immobile. They freeze everything and kill off life."

The next morning after breakfast he remains, as usual, sitting in his armchair, silent, apparently doing nothing, gazing into space. I am familiar with his exceptional ability to concentrate and know that he is capable of maintaining his watch for four or even five weeks at a time, waiting for inspiration to reawaken and a painting to come into his mind.

The rain falls, heavy, regular, abundant, but on the stroke of ten Bram suggests going out. So we set out on a walk that will take until midday.

"All this chatter, this confusion . . . All that's needed is a very few words, a few sentences."

I have to write a piece for the monograph the Galerie Maeght intends to publish on him, and I explain to him that—although I think I understand him—I am afraid that he may not recognize himself in the words I'll be obliged to use.

"It doesn't matter. You're not writing it for my sake. You must say what you have to say.

"It is difficult to find unknown phrases. Phrases that can welcome the unknown. It really seems as if painting or music are better able to express the unknown."

As on each occasion, I find that his concentration mobilizes, reunites, and focuses me, and that the ideas and sensations that emerge have an acuity that I owe to him. So, after weeks of fine weather, this first day of autumn rain recreates forgotten and refreshing states of mind. And I know that they wouldn't possess such clarity or intensity if I were not walking beside this man, with his extraordinary alertness to the least tremor of his internal being.

I feel a current passing between us again, and I yield to my old desire to question him about his childhood and past life, hoping that my devotion is clear enough for him not to think that I am prying.

He talks at some length about his father, a tormented man grappling with a demanding inner life (and I would remind the reader that all three of his children became artists). He also tells me about his mother, and the poverty in which they lived for so many years.

Then Bram talks about the play *Deafman Glance*, by the American Bob Wilson.[32] He hasn't seen it, but has read one or two reviews. He explains that it is the story of a boy who has witnessed his siblings' murders and been so traumatized by the event that he has been deaf ever since, living only through his eyes. Bram concludes:

"It's a bit like my own story . . .

"Once the eye has encountered horror, it sees it everywhere.

"My life is the story of the impossible becoming possible."

During his adolescence he was a passionate reader of the Russian classics, and also of Dickens. He read Knut Hamsun's book *Hunger*, which he has never forgotten because it relates an experience of destitution to some extent resembling his own. He read them, he says, less by choice than because they were published in cheap imprints and he could borrow them from the lending libraries.

Then he tells me about Worpswede, where he spent the least difficult two years of his entire life up to the age of sixty or more.

Then he talks about Paris:

"You have to play a role in life, to take on a part. I have never been able to do that.

"Sometimes it was a case of choosing between eating and buying a canvas.

"My life could be summed up as submitting to poverty without letting it destroy me.

"I have never tried to defend myself. And my painting is equally defenseless. I mean, you only have defenses if you live in the world of the intellect. To understand my painting, the intellect must be kept out of it.

"It's as if everyone constructs his own little refuge. What you have to do is survive without a refuge.

"I don't know what happened, but there have always been one or two people who took an interest in me. The funny thing is, they were never French. But they soon got tired of me. It's hard to help someone who does nothing to help himself.

"Always this poverty . . . But I never rebelled against it. I have always known that it was my place. And anyway, I had my work.

"Yes, I've had some incredible experiences. But always buoyed up by that fascinating little thing.

"Even failure isn't something you can seek.

"In a way, there was the satisfaction of not letting oneself be beaten.

"Well no, you mustn't believe that accepting being nothing makes one an exceptional person."

Then, as on every occasion, we talk about Beckett. At the time we're discussing, he had not yet had anything published in France, and he gave his manuscripts to Bram to read. Bram didn't always understand them very well, disconcerted as he was by the humor he found in them. He confides to me for the second time that the terrible Irish humor that Beckett exhibited had a quite astonishing power to lay things bare.

I also ask him about Jacques Putman, whom he met after the war.

"He helped me a great deal too. In the most disinterested way. In the beginning, he was like the American student faced with that Indian, Yaqui the shaman."[33]

The rain still hasn't let up. We return to the house and go to change our clothes and shoes. When I see him again I try to continue the conversation. He wards me off with his hands:

"No. There have been too many words already. Now, it's time to be quiet."

We sit down at table. During the meal, as usual, he is lost in himself, and when his eyes meet mine, he smiles awkwardly, as if to apologize.

After the meal, the conversation picks up again and I ask him why he sometimes feels ashamed when he is working.

"Well, because work is still an easy alternative, a means of escape.

"That's right. I have never really liked French painting. It's often too disciplined, too elegant. It is not genuine enough. It's as if art has got the upper hand."

When he lived in Paris, he preferred to go to the Louvre on Sundays, when it was most crowded—and I note the need for human contact felt by the solitary or by those who feel them-selves to be outcasts—and then only to see a few pictures: the Rembrandts, two Van Dycks, a Dutch landscape, a Goya, Tin-toretto's self-portrait, and *The Raft of the Medusa.*

We take the car and go off for a walk on the other side of town, in a park beside Lake Geneva. It is still raining. On my way over, I saw a signpost to the village where Simenon lives, and I talk to Bram about his journal.

"No doubt . . . But his mistake is that he has never demolished himself, he has always wanted to win. To get at the truth, you have to go through a process of destruction."

We set off on our walk, admiring the magnificent trees, the masses of flowers, the lake, the distant views . . .

And after a very long pause:

"But why is the truth so very well concealed?"

October 10, 1974

Walk with Jacques Putman. Inevitably, we talk about Bram. He tells me that Bram has been so scarred by his years of destitution that until very recently he was still living in fear of one day ending up in the workhouse.

Bram never has any money on him. Since his arrival in Switzerland, however, he and one particular fifty-franc note have been inseparable. A crumpled, faded, dog-eared note, which by now is almost falling apart. Bram frequently goes out for walks alone and is afraid of getting lost, so he wants to be able to take a taxi if he needs to.

Jacques talks about his eccentricity. About the way slightly odd things have always seemed to happen to him.

Before the war, in Montparnasse, Bram was associated with a group of artists from Central Europe. One of them later emigrated to the United States and ended up making a lot of money out there. In 1945, on his deathbed, he remembered Bram and his poverty and asked for his clothes to be sent to him. This was done, and explains how it came about that Bram—while living in utter destitution—went around in expensive clothes of unusual elegance at a time when the majority of people were poorly dressed.

"With him," Jacques added, "you can never be sure what's real, because basically he's never bothered much about it."

And he tells me how once, on leaving his house, Bram noticed a pair of glasses in a garbage can. He tried them on. They suited him, so he kept them for the next twenty years. But one day he had to go to see the optician. Jacques went with him. Eye test, glasses. Optician all amazement.

"But with glasses like these, you can't see anything at all."

And then, almost immediately:

"What sort of job do you do, anyway?"

Bram, noticing the trace of mockery in the man's astonishment, retorted magnificently:

"I paint my inner life."

December 30, 1974

As always in the winter, he is gloomy and disinclined to talk. But I realize from his obvious pleasure at seeing me again how alone he is, and how much he suffers from his isolation.

After the meal, we go out for what has become our customary walk. A gray day. Countryside devoid of life, but bordering the narrow road the ancient oak trees that we always admire. Bram is tense, anguished. Long, heavy silences. From time to time I hazard a question. Silence again. Then, several seconds later—sometimes stretching out to a minute, which seems endless—the answer springs from his lips. Brief, often incisive, uttered with impressive gravity and strength of conviction.

"What's lacking is reality.

"I am never really at ease except during the summer, in the garage (his workplace). There, I am truly naked.

"I have sought only to be free.

"I did what I did in order to be able to breathe. There is no merit in that. (Beckett said the same thing to me once, and I think in the very same words.)

"Working is first and foremost not doing anything.

"Most people's lives are a controlled routine. The artist is the person who seeks a life of liberty.

"When life appears, it is the unknown. But to be able to welcome the unknown, you have to be unencumbered.

"All that I have sought to do is not to betray life.

"In my work, I live my silence.

"The act has to be liberated.

"Doing has to include not-doing.

"Beauty is wonder at the unknown. But a true unknown.

"So many painters and writers never stop producing, because they are afraid of not-doing."

I talk a bit about myself. Tell him that I feel more settled. Less hungry for what may be going on elsewhere.

"Once you hit on your own adventure, you don't need all that nonsense anymore.

"Seeing is living the unknown.

"Why do something so pointless (i.e. painting)? Perhaps because it redeems everything else.

"So many works are devoid of mystery."

I talk about the intermittency of life. About the periods I go through when I completely dry up.

"When life is absent, you have to know how to abstain. Those who force themselves to act fail to understand that they are condemning themselves to a lie.

"I had to express all that is wretched in life, all those things to which people have generally shut their eyes.

"I am a primitive. I had to unearth the vital element."

I ask him what painting has given him.

"It has allowed me not to be a complete washout."

April 4, 1975

He is suffering from his isolation. He has talked about it several
times. As always during the winter, he has been unable to work.
He has seen nobody. He goes out walking or sits for hours in his
armchair, entirely given over to what is taking shape inside him.
He talks frequently about the unknown, of what emerges when
all desire, all will and self-regard have spontaneously vanished
and the being becomes purely passive. It is to the extent that he
has the audacity and courage to welcome the unknown that the
painter can engender something new and produce paintings
which are each an effective encounter with life.

"Painting, he says, is attempting to reach a point where it is
impossible to remain."

That evening over dinner he is in good form and tells us about
Holland, and about his days in Worpswede (in 1922, when he
was 27). He refers to the piece by Thomas de Quincey in which
he tells how Descartes was almost dispatched to the other world
by the very people he had engaged to help him cross the Zuyder
Zee.[34] We talk briefly about Descartes but a dispute arises and,
to settle it, we refer to an encyclopedia. I read out the entry on
Descartes and eventually get to the famous statement "I think,
therefore I am."

Bram interrupts, bursting out:

"No no. He was wrong. He should have said, 'I think, therefore
I collapse.'"

For the rest of the evening he talks with great feeling about
Kollmar, a painter of German origin, who was at Worpswede at

the same time as himself.[35] He had lived for some years in China before returning to Germany and starting to paint. He may even have had psychiatric problems. In order to rest and be in an environment conducive to work, he had then moved to this small village with its colony of resident artists.

He was lordly in appearance and manner and was in fact a visionary, *a person gifted with terrifying lucidity*, Bram says. In many respects, he was a similar sort of person to Artaud. People loathed him because he frightened them. But Bram sought his company. He could complete a canvas in a very short time, or talk for two or three hours on end, advancing brilliant propositions that later turned out to be prophetic. Bram has never met anyone so fascinating. And, trying to make us understand what he was like, Bram comes out with this phrase:

"You could see him burn."

May 1, 1975

"Why the shame? Because these days there aren't so many reasons left to celebrate life. Everything is collapsing around us.

"I paint to kill off the word.

"Even if you can't see it, you have to realize that you live in a
criminal world. Everything is designed to kill off life.

"Life is constantly being falsified. Painting is an attempt to get
at the truth.

"It is terrible to be tied to life. Every instant is a battle."

In the morning, on waking, I sit and read by myself for awhile
before hearing that he is up and has been outside for quite some
time. I go to join him. Sitting down beside him, I savor the magnificent day that is beginning. Dazzling light. Freshness and
warmth. The smell of cut grass. Masses of flowers. And the wil-
low. And the tall birch trees. And the birdsong.

I turn to Bram. And stop, openmouthed. I have never seen him
in such a state.

A few days ago, the triennial Prix de la Revue de Belles-Lettres
was awarded to him, and this prize is to be presented in three
weeks time during a little ceremony to be held at the Château de
Rolle.

The cause of his present anguish is that he will have to say a few
words in public.

"You must come. You can give a speech for me. You can thank
them. I've never been able to speak. Everything I had to say went
into my painting."

And, distraught, with tears in his eyes:

"Having no words makes you a cripple. It's made my life a calvary."

A squirrel is playing around the foot of a tree.

I was dumbfounded, but had I been able to speak, I should have tried to convince Bram that he uses words better than anybody. To tell him that, if he can't take part in ordinary conversation and feels unable to express himself, it is simply because he only manages to speak when he has to formulate something relating to the fundamental. And that the great problems of communication which have afflicted him all his life probably result less from an inability to use words than from the imperious desire for authenticity that possesses him.

August 8-10, 1975

For the last two months he has been painting and experiencing that mixture of happiness, anxiety, and fatigue which invariably marks a period of work. It is he who insists that we should stay for three days. It will give him a break, a chance to get his strength back.

"The canvas is really a battle.

"It is vital to see.

"To see is really to be without prior knowledge.

"It's a sad story. Painting scares me, and yet I have to paint."

I talk to him about fear. Tell him that it has always seemed to me to be at the root of all that we are. We are in the garage, so he shows me the three gouaches he has just finished, which are pinned to the wall.

"They express all that.

"You feel great dread when you set out to encounter the unknown."

Recently, visiting a collector, he saw a painting he had forgotten.

"I was frightened. I was rooted to the spot."

A moment later, in response to a remark from me:

"You have to take care to go unnoticed. Not to attract attention to yourself.

"When I am working, everything I've done comes back and goes into my hand. Instead of being behind me, it's suddenly in front.

"But it is the unknown that has to emerge. Only that."

I refer to the great examples of Titian and Tintoretto.

"Yes, they could do it. They lived a kind of absolute. But now it's much more difficult."

He tells me about the extreme difficulty he experiences in painting, due to his complete ignorance of what it is that is crying out to take shape on the canvas.

Later, we are talking about those literary works of the past that indisputably contain the truth but which are, for us, a dead letter. And as I remark on the rarity of those works that encompass what needs to be revealed and kept in circulation from one mind to another, he observes:

"You have to recognize that art has only very rarely served the cause of truth.

"There is undeniably a source of truth, but you have to seek it out."

I talk about those people who live as if cut off from themselves, without any real communication with their most secret and intimate selves.

"Yes, it is a tragedy, all these people who never encounter their life."

Then we return to the subject of the solitude of the artist. The rejection he experiences. This society, which is bound to reject what he is and what he spends his time trying to express. And he adds, his face shadowed by sudden melancholy:

"The many powers of untruth and the extreme weakness of truth, that's the tragedy."

December 6, 1975

A friend of mine, Jean-François Delaunay, has been to visit him. Bram was happy to see him, glad to have someone to talk to.

And displaying his most recent gouaches:

"These are my latest paroxysms."

He has told him about his life in Paris during the war, when he was without family or friends, cold and hungry and unable to work.

"I could carry on because my hope was focused elsewhere."

Before the war, Marthe Arnaud's *Manières de Blanc* was serialized in *l'Humanité*.[36] (Bram's first acquaintance with this woman, who was one day to become his companion, dated back to 1936. She had previously been a Protestant nun and worked as a missionary on the Zambezi. While there, she became aware of the implications of the presence and activities of the whites in black Africa and began to reconsider her own role. She began to listen to the blacks and learn about their culture. This led her to write her book *Manières de Blanc*, which elicited messages of support from Le Corbusier, Romain Rolland, Lévy-Brühl, and others.) She became the victim of police harassment. One day when she was ill and in bed, some policemen turned up to question her, and Bram had the greatest difficulty in persuading them to leave her in peace. In the end, the police left but served a summons on them both.

Bram and Marthe presented themselves at the police station at the right time on the appointed day and found themselves in a bare room, facing a policeman who was busy typing, deliberately ignoring them. Bram took a few steps and glanced out of the window. In the station yard, a parade was going on and dozens of uniformed policemen were lined up like so many lead soldiers. Struck by the sight of all the blue against the white walls, Bram exclaimed:

"Marthe, Marthe, come and see. It's a study in blue."

Bram spoke with such conviction that the policeman stopped typing to get up and look out of the window. Bewilderment. Without further ado, in an expressionless voice, he told them to go.

"You see," Madeleine breaks in, "once again, it's painting that saved you."

December 28, 1975

A spirit forever wounded, lacerated, tortured by doubt, suffering from his solitude. A fine exhibition is showing at the Galerie Maeght, the monograph about him has just appeared, but nothing seems to give him any pleasure or banish the memory of the suffering he endured during his years of destitution. I have never seen him so depressed.

In the evening, over our meal—laughing all the time, because he hasn't lost his sense of humor—he tells me how once, well before the war, he went up to Montmartre where it was at that time the custom for painters of all sorts to come on Sundays to exhibit their paintings in the Place du Tertre. Bram strolls around looking at the paintings, then, just as he's leaving, comes across a painter who has taken up position in a side street. His canvases are spread out on the pavement and he explains to Bram that he is only there because he can't afford to pay the small fee charged to "exhibit" in the square itself. Bram likes his naïve paintings, takes a liking to the man himself, and—since he has a bit of money on him and the paintings are for sale for next to nothing—buys two of them. The stranger whose signature they bear is called Camille Bombois.

Some years go by. One day, an art fancier turns up at his studio on the recommendation of friends. Bram is in dire straits and would be glad of the chance to sell, but the visitor is not at all enthused by his work. He is about to leave when he suddenly notices the two canvases by Camille Bombois. He offers to buy them. Bram, who's practically out on the street, doesn't wait to be asked twice, and hands them over. A few days later, he learns that he could have got five times what he asked for them.

Later in the evening:

"Anyone seeking life has to put up a terrible battle against this system that kills off life.

"The incredible thing is that there is nothing, and then suddenly the possibility of seeing emerges. Yes, it's true, you can see."

He identifies vision with life, and I can understand that. For it is when the spirit is reduced to the eye, pure vision, that it experiences with greatest intensity.

"That little thing, nothing can make it come. You just have to wait and do nothing."

And after a long pause, in a tone of voice tinged with rage:

"All security should be destroyed."

He has this amazing combination of the most incisive lucidity and a boundless innocence and naivety. In Beckett, too, I was struck by the same combination of strength, lucidity, and exceptional spiritual power existing side by side with qualities that very rarely survive in their shade: gentleness, passiveness, and vulnerability.

March 27, 1976

Just back from three days in Geneva with Bram.

The first day, beautiful weather, a long walk. He tells me things about his mother, his father, about Marthe Arnaud. He complains of his solitude and isolation. The last six months have again been very difficult.

"Why do you read the papers?"

"It's a way of being in touch with life. Of rubbing up against the dreadfulness.

"The will very soon reveals its limits.

"You have to let not-working do its work.

"I don't believe in the solution but I do believe in the effort."

I talk about Mondrian. But he objects:

"Purity is often pretty dirty. There are so many people who strike sublime attitudes."

I am deeply interested in these issues and have given them a lot of thought. Using an entirely different vocabulary, wouldn't I be likely to write that Mondrian identifies himself with the demands of the universal and yet aims to express nothing more than his need for order, unity, peace, and harmony, while Bram—experiencing the same demands—can report only on his struggle, his efforts, and his failures? Mondrian paints our aspiration to the immense and unconditional, and Bram the drama of our inability to live up to the full implications of that aspiration.

I continue to question him.

"You have to allow yourself to be destroyed.

"It is terrible to have to carry on a solitary struggle.

"Art in France? It is often moderation. The mastery of moderation. It never tries to expand the limits of apparent possibility.

"Without going to meet the unknown, there is no life. He constantly insists on the necessity of not-wanting and not-acting."

We talk at length about Beckett. He is full of admiration at the simplicity he has attained.

"To see life, you have to be detached. The point of it all is only apparent from the outside.

"Art is not something you can learn.

"In this world, you have to prove yourself all the time. But in the area into which we have to venture, there are no proofs.

"Artaud? He was a person who never shrank from life."

The next day, we go for a forest walk in the Jura. The path climbs up beside a narrow mountain stream boiling with wild, foaming water. Magnificent view over Lake Geneva and, in the far distance, the snow-covered Alps.

We emerge from the woods and continue our walk along the road.

We talk. Once again I become aware of his solitude, the tragedy at the heart of his life.

"So many threats hang over what the artist is trying to do. The whole world conspires to destroy his quest.

"Fear has been the engine behind everything I have done.

"It is terribly difficult to get close to nothingness.

"Something must be captured. If not, there's no life in it."

In the evening, over dinner, we talk about Chardin, Millet, Corot . . .

"Yes, each of those painters is a page from life."

Then he talks about Holland. He draws a parallel between Holland and Russia, explaining that the vast expanse of land and sky crush humanity while at the same time constantly confronting people with the infinite and kindling a nameless thirst in them. Hence the indefinable amalgam of melancholy and a desire to be elsewhere. Laughing, he concludes:

"Holland is like a Russia that hasn't got round to having its revolution."

Still the same beautiful weather the next day. I postpone our departure and, once again, we go out walking.

"It's a long time since there's been any point in painting pictures that are beautiful in the traditional sense of the word. It's not easy to produce a picture which is bad but still gives you satisfaction."

It is months since he has produced anything.

"I am always on the track of something. But there's no life in it.

"When I paint, I have to recapture the life force."

Yes, looking at his gouaches, you feel life flowing, gushing, pouring, streaming through them. He frequently talks about non-fatigue.

During the war, he went five years without being able to paint. He wandered around the streets endlessly or sat in his studio, doing nothing, staring at his paintings on the walls.

And he adds, with arresting gravity:

"They gave me life."

I mention a particular writer, and he concludes:

"You have to avoid careerism."

Once again, he explains how close he feels to Baudelaire. We talk about Beckett, the man and his work. And he tells me how Beckett came to be stabbed by a tramp.

He returns to the subject of Holland. Tells me more about his father, describing him as a real Dostoyevskian hero. Then he talks at length about Marthe Arthaud, to whom he was very attached.

"She was a gentle, lively person," he explains, "who still had something childlike about her . . . She had experienced disaster . . . She was very noble, very detached . . . You see, she was a non-calculating person . . . And people like that always get destroyed."

May 27-28, 1976

After six to eight months of inactivity, he has just produced a gouache. It is still out in the garage, and that's where we go to look at it.

"I prefer gouache to oils. It flows more. I have more flexibility and freedom."

When I observe that he is getting better and better at painting badly, he adds:

"I have to move towards this primitive life. Otherwise, there's nothing."

Primitivism of form and color. A somber vehemence. Tensions. Struggle. Painting of this kind challenges the ascendancy of reason, knowledge, the will, logic, certainty, and intellectual decision-making.

During our afternoon walk:

"Most people get themselves onto a single track just as soon as they can and never get off it again. I'm different. I've never had a track. I have always been feeling my way.

"A painting has to be a record of life.

"Life is our only asset.

"I am held prisoner by my eyes."

October 30, 1976

I arrive in Zurich in the late afternoon and go to the Galerie Maeght, where an exhibition of Bram's latest work opened yesterday.

The three gouaches he painted this summer seem to me the best. You feel a real pleasure in painting in them, and the joy that suffuses the forms and colors is becoming ever more tangible. But I understand the difficulty he confronts in his work: the gouache must give the impression of being no more than a rough sketch, for how else can he accurately reproduce that magma which is always on the move and is clearly, by its very nature, impossible to capture? But at the same time, it is vital that the gouache should not appear to be unfinished, that it should express power and fulfillment and the jubilation that presides over this attempt to grasp life in its totality.

Of the seven major one-man shows or retrospectives of Bram's work that I have had the opportunity of visiting, this is the one that has affected me most. But I couldn't say whether my response is due to the quality of the works on display or simply to my preference for this particular gallery. It's true that I liked having to go downstairs to find the pictures. I had an instant impression of buried treasure, then, immediately afterwards, of intimacy. The feeling of being underground, in a realm of peace and silence far removed from the city and its bustle, produced an immediate concentration that allowed me to enter into a genuine dialogue with the paintings.

In the evening, after eating out, our little party wandered back through the streets of the old town. As always when I find myself in Zurich or in Basel, or in any of the German towns around Lake Constance, my thoughts turn to Meister Eckhart, to Suso and Tauler, to Dürer or Holbein, or to some character in Marguerite Yourcenar's *The Abyss* . . .

The next day, towards midday, I meet Bram at the gallery. We talk at length.

"My painting is bound up with the phenomenon we call seeing. What do we mean by seeing, since we never do see?"

We inspect his gouaches. He confides to me that, seeing them here, it's as if he has never seen them before (and knowing him, I can well believe it). He admits that he can say nothing about them, can give no explanation or commentary. He tells me that, since what he has to show is not something that can be represented, he is anxious to produce a painting that cannot be approached rationally, through words and the usual points of reference. He wishes to reconstruct the unknown, while preserving that powerful sense of the alien that it possesses when it first erupts into our consciousness.

He talks again about Baudelaire and his perpetual search for truth.

His admiration for Rembrandt.

"His paintings are charged with such mystery. They are mystery itself. And yet, there is never anything supernatural in them."

In the early afternoon, I go to the Museum to visit a Turner exhibition. Bram has seen it two days ago. Returning to the hotel, we have some time to kill before needing to leave for the station, and I discuss it with him.

He dislikes Turner's early dramatic landscapes. He explains that Turner's vision remained superficial, proceeding merely from the eye and what the eye grasps of the exterior world.

I refer to a particular painting of a sunset.

"Yes, of course it's beautiful . . . You can't deny that . . . But it's so far from what we're called upon to accomplish . . . What life offers is so much greater than all the pleasures and happinesses we could ever imagine."

April, 1977

After having lived with M. for 17 years, Bram had to flee Geneva in a panic, leaving everything behind him. He returned to Paris, to live with Jacques and Catherine, who welcomed him. He is somber, tense, and I had to convince him to give me this interview, intended for a radio show.

With the microphone barely set up, he starts off right away, releasing the pressure inside him. His delivery is jerky, his voice filled with emotion:

"True decisive steps are necessarily rare . . . A painting, a true painting, is a marvel, you can live it . . . It's not about producing more and more. I did what I could . . . I was always afraid, I don't know, it scares me . . . Painting, facing it, carrying all of that around scares me . . . I live it, knowing full well how dangerous it is . . . but I have to remain the master . . . In fact, it's all the same story . . . What is a painting? . . . The story of painting is an abominable one . . . I'm a man who lives in fear of the real world, which threatens me, and against which I have no defenses . . . The painting, which all of this experience goes into, frees me from it. It's a glorious moment . . . I live for that sort of moment! Only to fall into fear again afterward."

He stops. I have the impression he thinks he's said everything, that he has nothing more to add. The interview would be finished there, before it had begun. He is closed in on himself, grappling with his suffering, with what he hasn't stopped brooding about since losing his partner. Is there anything I can ask him that won't put us in an awkward position? Despite my doubts, I try to re-launch the interview.

"Before we get to your work, I'd like you to tell me about your life, about the road you've traveled. We can specify that you were born in Holland, near Leyde, in Zoeterwoude, in 1895, and that you grew up in Holland."

"Yes, but can I add something? We left Leyde for La Haye, and that's where I lived throughout my entire childhood."

"Do you still have memories of your childhood?"

"I remember the part of my life when I was a painter's apprentice very well, basically a house painter. But there was also a decorative part of the work. They saw that I had talent and they asked me to design and paint lampshades."

"And furniture as well?"

"We worked in rich people's houses. They'd station several painters in a house, and after several months, the place would be completely inhabitable."

"Would you tell me about the kind of child you were?"

"My childhood was destitute. My father was a very miserable man. He couldn't stand living at our house, so he left. My mother stayed with four children and she had to support them herself, so it was a very hard life . . . But I always wanted to be a painter . . ."

"Even as a child, you already had the idea?"

"When I was seven I was given colored pencils and I made a drawing of a windmill. And people thought it was beautiful, at least in my family circle . . . well, I never gave up the idea of being a painter. And it stayed with me. Up til today."

"When you showed this drawing to your father, he was struck by it, wasn't he?"

"Yes, exactly, the first drawing I did, that windmill I invented on the spot . . . I had seen them often . . . but I drew it on the spot, like a revelation, I still almost work like that today, I never know what kind of painting will come out. It's always diving into a world that I haven't seen yet. I have to see it."

"To make it exist?"

"Yes, it's in me, but I have to see it, and there are some wonderful moments when I manage it. By continuing on this track, I have been able to live through some incredible moments, incredible spaces and times, because it's true, painting contains possibilities that we don't understand, and in living our life—even when middle-aged—it's still a discovery."

"In fact, you are essentially an inwardly oriented man."

"I don't know about that, but the surprising thing, the surprising thing for me, is that each time a painting comes to me, I don't recognize it, I don't see it happening. The act of painting is a sort of despair, a despair that you sink into, but that you know nothing about, except that it's a nightmare."

"It's plunging into the unknown."

"Yes, but once you're there, it's as though it was always there, I mean, it's not imaginary, it's something completely natural, it was always there."

"You're a man of silence and solitude, and it's precisely to give what's inside you the best chance to be born that you're quiet so often. Because you often stay silent for hours and hours, without moving, meditating, essentially focused on whatever is happening inside you."

"I am attentive to a sort of life inside me, and the painting I've done helps me to follow this road . . . I wait calmly . . . or else in agony . . . for another opportunity to arise, because that is my real life. Even looking at paintings done years ago, many years ago, there is a great pleasure in the act of seeing, so it's really a joy to see, which is essential. I don't think I'm explaining this well, but I'm not trying very hard to correct myself, because seeing and speaking are two completely different things."

"Opposites, even . . ."

"Yes, I think so . . . yes, I think that the man seeing is the true man. While the man speaking . . . usually there's no truth to him."

"What is striking when one meets you is the fact that you shy away from words so much. I mean that you don't let your words interfere. They aren't a barrier when you face the unknown that rises up in you. You are in a state of total innocence: there are no words, there is no formulation, there is no mental representation."

"I have to run away from speech. Painting is the act in which I am running away, in which I'm no longer in danger, in which the danger has passed . . . because, like everyone, I live in a state of constant danger."

"Do you sometimes feel that you've distanced yourself from the same intensity of life that you're searching for?"

"Yes, there are moments, periods when I don't dare to work, I can't, I don't have any light in me."

"You don't have the energy."

"Yes."

"Are these periods difficult for you, painful?"

"That's the most difficult thing there is: to hover in a state where you can't do anything."

"And you can't just try to work to get yourself started . . ."

"No, that's the hardest thing, you don't have the courage to act, you float . . . You float and you can't act . . ."

"You once told me, 'I'm getting better and better at painting badly.' I think we could say that when you were in your twenties you were able to paint like Rembrandt. You made copies of Rembrandt paintings and they could even be confused with the originals. So you moved away from this savoir faire progressively to adapt your medium to what you wanted to express."

"Yes, at first it was beginner's work, apprentice work. Afterwards, it was something completely different. It wasn't about seeing what's shown in museums, but what one sees in life."

"When you went to Worpswede in 1922, you were already on this track?"

"Sort of. The Worpswede period helped me to see what life is, helped me to stop looking for it in museums. Afterwards, in Paris, I was still going through the same evolution. I started, slowly, to see myself . . . until I reached those very intense moments, those moments of collapse, when I no longer knew anything at all."

"Yes, you've told me that when you finished a painting, you sometimes didn't even know where you were."

"Yes, I experienced a very strange thing, very powerful, and it kept me alive for weeks and weeks afterwards, I was being carried along by the completed object, which accompanied me everywhere. And it's in this sort of state that one sees, how should I put it, that everything is inside of you, that there is no outside, so you lose your footing, you're not in the outside world anymore."

"But, to be precise, returning to that world can be a painful process."

"Oh, there's always that friction with the real world, but you can't really bring yourself to hate it, it's always there. A painting represents the moment when the world disappeared, but it often takes weeks to bring oneself to that point. Those moments are rescues, who knows how it happens . . . one is saved because one has forgotten oneself."

"You've told me many times that, for you, work comes by way of non-work."

"Yes, yes, that's something I told a woman who wanted me to contribute to her catalogue. We talked a little and I came up with this phrase: that work comes by way of non-work. Because, and this is what's marvelous, in a real painting, both work and non-work are there. It's an image, but also a non-image . . . Basically, a painting is something that eludes me, it's the other, it's as if a person were two people, and one side had to rejoin the other. If a painting really is this plunge that one was able to take, then it's there that one can see the other. One is liberated, and these are the things that never leave you . . . they stay with you."

"Were you always this kind of painter? When you were thirty-five, forty . . ."

"Yes, I think I always had a little of this, even when I was doing other things, things that could be, how should I put it, easily named, there was already a little bit of this."

"Do you find it easier to live in these states of mind, now?"

"Oh, right now, I'm going through a very hard time . . . It still happens that . . . that the thing that can come isn't coming."

"Yes, but you've always had long periods of aridity, or of great internal silence, and you've never, I think, panicked?"

"Yes, but it can still get very bad, I go weeks when I can't get anything done . . . How miraculous it is to be able to do something!"

"And obviously, you can't *make* anything happen—you can't do anything to encourage the right thing to come?"

"No, no, it's very a complicated thing, a sort of revelation."

"You once told me, 'It is through misery that I have got closer to *life*.' I think that the very difficult childhood that you had, and then the difficult years you lived in Paris, before and particularly during the war, have obviously influenced you very strongly."

"The main thing is that one be bold enough to act. When doubt becomes too strong, one isn't able to be that bold anymore . . . and that's an awful thing."

"You've always been after the truth?"

"A painting lives because of one's courage in facing the un-known—it's an act of courage. And yet, often, one doesn't have this absolute courage, it's decreased, or disappeared . . . Life crushes many things . . ."

"You have a very sharp sense of what life is."

"That is, I have a sense of where life is and where non-life is."

"And life is . . ."

"Life, for me, is true, and non-life is false."

"Artaud said, 'I feel so much bitterness in existing falsely.' And I think that's what happens when . . ."

"Truth saves . . . truth is the act that saves . . ."

"Inside you, during all those hours that you spend in solitude, there is always this silent pursuit . . . All those hours are your means of approaching the truth, of what you feel to be true, that is, of that place where life is most intense. Your whole existence has been dominated by this pursuit, by this need, and I think that if one wants to talk about your painting, one essentially needs to approach it from this angle. You are someone who has always looked for life."

"Sometimes there are no words, there is only hesitation . . ."

"You've often told me, 'The important thing is to be nothing.' Thus to have no will, no desire of any kind, so as not to stand in the way of whatever is trying to be born."

"Yes, I've put my life into my paintings. But maybe one empties oneself as well. Maybe one isn't filling oneself, maybe one is being emptied . . ."

"And yet when people see the gouaches you've produced these last few years, they get the impression more of a great stream of life, don't they?"

"Sometimes the finished thing doesn't manage to show you that there, right in front of you, is nothing."

"Do you feel you're gaining life from the paintings you've completed these last few years? Do they give you life?"

"I am very much linked to what I've done, but it doesn't move me forward. Before, there was a sort of . . ."

"Non-life . . . ?"

"One lives in the invisible, and that's the only way to see, otherwise there's no life. If one isn't able to show what's inside of oneself . . . It's strange . . . I can't talk about it clearly . . . A hidden life that comes out . . ."

"What happens when you see your paintings in an exhibition?"

"An exhibition, yes—if I see my work in a very unexpected way, as sometimes happens, then I'm happy . . . others talk about unhappiness, distress, but I am happy. Because then it's as though such fragile life still had a chance to be . . ."

"A painting is really a kind of putting into image-form what is happening inside of you."

"You have to see yourself. You finally see what you have become. A painting is what one has become."

"To really understand your paintings, one can't forget that what you're trying to show is always in motion. That's why you told me that your paintings can't be frozen in place. To respect this movement of life. You confided to me, one day, 'I am a liquid being.'"

"Yes, there's no solidity in any of it. Everything is fragile, everything is . . ."

"In fact, a painting is always a bit of a preliminary sketch."

"A state where one approaches one's true life, which is very much a state of insecurity. It's amazing that one can manage to see into this state, where nothing is fixed, where it's as though everything is floating. There's probably an entire hidden life inside our heads. The painter has to show it . . . thus, painting is a safe place from which we can venture toward the unknown."

"That's how the act of painting relates to others. Because the act itself is a pursuit of life."

"Yes, it's a world to discover and never know . . . Always to discover . . . Painting has the power to leave the real world behind, and then, there, one can finally breathe, one lives one's real life, it's miraculous . . ."

April 25, 1977—Paris

Just over a week ago, I spent two days with him in Geneva. We went to see the De Kooning exhibition at the Cabinet des Estampes, and then walked for an hour or two in the park beside the lake. Like today, he had a lot to say. But the person who spoke to me that day was not the painter but the private individual, and for that reason I would rather not commit his confidences to paper.

We had lunch at Jacques's house, just the two of us together, in complete silence. Then we went up to his room for a moment. The only belongings he has there are the slim volumes of Beckett's latest work, sent to him by Beckett himself.

I see for the first time a picture he painted just after the war, in which he tried to express the darkness and violence of the time.

"We lived like ghosts."

Then, a moment later, in response to a question from me:

"It has always been more important to me to do nothing than to do something."

We go for a walk in the Jardin du Luxembourg, and he leads me to the statue of Sainte-Beuve which he mentioned recently and which I couldn't find the day before yesterday. Then he lures me on a little further and has the fun of surprising me with the beehives that are there, and for a few minutes we stand and listen, hands behind our backs, to a lesson on beekeeping being given by a teacher to a small group of youngsters.

That evening, Jacques and Catherine[37] are taking him to visit Beaubourg for the first time, to see the two paintings of his that are on permanent exhibition there, and they kindly invite me to go with them.

Afterwards, dinner in a restaurant with some of Bram's lithos on the walls. He is silent, tense, anguished, sometimes absent.

Then we go outside. The gentle warmth of a marvelous spring evening and Paris all lit up. We walk home in a silence broken only at one point when, with Notre-Dame and the view of the bridges and quays in front of us, we pause to enjoy the spectacle and he tells me how much he is enjoying renewing his acquaintance with this city, which he adores.

November 7, 1977—Paris

Over the last few days, I have had three meetings with him.

In his room, with his most recent gouaches. They are exceedingly good! Ample, rich, intense, tragic yet joyful, moving, mysterious . . . All the suffering he has endured over the last few months is there for all to see on these sheets of paper, in these colors and forms . . .

He has also produced two large gouaches: one black and white and the other, also black, but with a broad expanse of white and some streaks of pale orange. When I speak of the power and the feeling of tragedy that his paintings exude, he observes:

"I have tried to put my whole self into them."

The next day we look at them again with Jacques, Catherine, and one of their friends, and—when Bram leaves the room for a moment—Jacques points out to us how minimal the materials he uses have become: his equipment, in its entirety, consists of a rickety little table bearing three brushes, a dish of red, a dish of black, the two corresponding tubes of paint, a tube of white, a bottle of Indian ink, and, leaning against the wall, a sheet of plywood.

Today we had lunch together at Jacques's house, then set out for a walk. We crossed the Pont-Neuf and went down onto the quay where he usually goes to walk. There was a bench free and we sat there for almost two hours, with the glorious late-autumn sun on our faces. The barges, the lapping water, the light sparkling on the waves, the lovers strolling by, holding hands—and the city with all its noise and bustle.

"I am destroyed by the incomprehensible.

"Painting is what has given me relief from the worst.

"You always feel guilty.

"Being no more than a puppet . . . It's hard to live a life of self-effacement."

He explains that he has never been able to like art that is assertive and self-assertive. Tells me he has read and reread *Footfalls*, Beckett's latest piece.

And, shaking his head, with a broad smile in which I can decipher wonder, incredulity, and a trace of the affection in which he holds Beckett:

"To derive so much life from such ruins . . ."

A lengthy silence. There is something I want to say to him, but I don't know quite how to put it. I can't find the right words. At last, I get it out:

"You know, Bram, when you consider the tragic life stories of some painters and poets, you get the feeling that things couldn't have been any other way, that what they went through was absolutely necessary. And when I think about you, I come more or less to the same conclusion in the end. Don't you think that your recent catastrophe[38] is part of your destiny, part of the suffering that's always accompanied you?"

He raises his head and gazes out thoughtfully over the Seine for a few seconds.

"Occasionally, over the last few weeks, I have wondered about that.

"This shock has thrown the whole of my work and life into question again.

"When there is no understanding around you, there is nothing.

"Where misery leads you . . ."

A long silence. To divert his thoughts, I return to the subject of painting.

"The act of painting," he replies, "is at once inevitable and completely inexplicable.

"The visible world scares me. I am always trying to escape. It is only when I have a canvas in front of me that I don't run away.

"There must be no model.

"In the beginning, I painted ridiculous pictures. I thought painting was a matter of imitating the pictures in the museums.

"Such an aspiration to life that the entire spirit is committed to it."

Then he tells me how what goes on in his mind seems to him so strange that he cannot bring himself to put it into words. Whenever he is tempted to do so, he has such a feeling of betrayal and of failure that he prefers to keep silent.

"Words are a massacre.

"Only the void and the world of silence are immense."

And, a few minutes later:

"When you accede to the sublime, it's so wonderful."

We go home. Crossing back over the Pont-Neuf, he clutches my arm. With his free hand he gestures at the Seine, the bridges, the beauty of the scene, wordlessly inviting me to savor the sumptuous light already dying away over the city even as we watch.

Yes, to turn back. To reverse the impulse that drives us to expend ourselves on the outside world, to turn it to our advantage, to seize it in our talons. To direct our gaze inward and allow it to search the same eye from which it emanates. To seek a place upstream of our source and, once there, to try to become our own cause. Or, rather, to work to annihilate ourselves, and then to crawl, to re-ascend, to cross the valley and find again the warm waters of our origins.

But to acquiesce to this need to rediscover our initial bliss—this yearning which burns in the very depths of our blood—is in no way, as people say, to regress, to abandon ourselves to the uncontrolled forces of the unconscious or to renounce thought, reflection, or awareness. This desire to plunge back into the world before birth is, at the same time, an acceptance of the necessity of penetrating the dullness and opacity of the ego, of bursting its bounds, escaping its constraints, striving to achieve a liberty in which the spirit can at last open itself up to life entirely and submit to the law that enjoins it to strive toward an ever greater strength, awareness, intensity, and light. And so, to turn back is to devote ourselves to engendering ourselves, to creating a new being issuing directly from our craving for, if not our condition of, complete liberty. (That sovereign peace to which we aspire, and which we could achieve if we were only able to heal the rift of fragmentation and duality, we identify, no doubt, with that never-forgotten peace that we experienced before the fall. Hence our desire to curl up again within the womb fuses with our need to create in ourselves, by the sole power of interior elucidation, that immensity where the spirit, overflowing with energy, can savor the fulfillment of unity regained and, shrugging off all restrictions, surrender itself to the most vast and intense jubilation.)

As Hölderlin noted: "He who has thought most profoundly, loves what is most alive."[39] We may come closer to what is being described here if we reverse this proposition to read, for example: "He who loves what is most alive, cannot help but think most profoundly."

Those who strive to reach their source, the original state of bliss, what is most alive, find themselves led to clear the decks, to denude themselves, to explore every nook and cranny of the self, and—by so doing—to lay the foundations of effective knowledge.

To think most profoundly is, therefore, to ensure that the eye of consciousness scrutinizes what constitutes itself, and what directs and governs its vision. It is to ensure that the spirit unceasingly probes its own depths, penetrating ever further into itself and freeing itself of its fears, its egocentricity, and its constraints. And it is to ensure that the greatest possible part of the unconsciousness yields up its secrets, that the most subtle mechanisms of the psyche are laid bare, and that thought—thereby acceding to the domain of the neutral and universal—knows no further impediments, no barriers and no taboos.

Emptiness, the ebb and flow of superabundance, the unending cycle, the high swell and surge of light . . .

Works to which we come to drink in the most alive, to encounter those who have *thought most profoundly*, are therefore those that recount or reveal the slow, painful, costly pilgrimage of a spirit resolutely journeying back towards its source. Such odysseys of the insatiable soul are tragic. They happen also to be rare. But the works of Bram van Velde are among their number.

Those who are driven by an inner compulsion, as Hölderlin has it elsewhere, to seek "but one thing: the greatest and most beautiful,"[40] are generally condemned to experience nothing but disappointment, bitterness, and despair. For the object of their ardor is withheld, or reveals itself only in sudden illuminations, when the spirit is closest to nothingness and finds itself summoned to the places of deepest desolation and most productive wells of profound silence. And the worst is that the object of the quest imposes the renunciation of knowledge, of action, and of will. A crushing demand!

Forced to journey onwards towards an ever more distant goal, obliged to trust itself to passive waiting, such a spirit wanders endlessly in arid, featureless lands, sunk in a murky, sunless gloom.

Brother to Beckett, to Molloy, traveling without respite towards his mother, Bram van Velde has recorded, on his canvases, the nature of his fate, of the warp and weft of his life, of all our lives, by which I mean the ontological frustration, that unassuageable thirst, the radical state of deprivation—the blocked, the precarious, the inert, the enervated, the vicious, the trembling, the dismayed, the naked, the infirm, the vacillating, the dispossessed, the exiled, the inconsolable . . .

Hence his harsh, mournful, tragic paintings, the complete sincerity of which stimulates and challenges us.

Paintings sometimes filled to the limit, but which nevertheless—when we learn how to read them, to let them permeate our consciousness—convey a profound silence. (It took me a very long time to grasp and understand and finally to appreciate this savage, distraught, vehement kind of painting, which offers us a glimpse of the inner magma—as it were—with all its heterogeneity, its tensions, tumult, and stagnancies, and of the currents that traverse and torment it, seeking to impose peace, organization, and unity. And if I say that I was struck by this amazing silence, it's not because of any autosuggestion on my part: it really did impress itself upon me. Silence of that kind bears witness to the fact that what the artist has captured on his canvas issues from what is most profound and universal in us all. Hence, it removes the image from the realm of the particular and individual and transforms it into a mirror in which we can all recognize ourselves.) The paintings convey a joyful serenity, a lightness, an assuaging transparency, and, very often, the suggestion of a circle, demonstrating the presence of the opposite pole and indicating a nearness to the hoped-for unity, a moment when the spirit has almost stumbled into the infinite.

These paintings, which express our essential deprivation, deprive us of nothing. With their rough, uncertain, secretly ordered structures, their dull, dirty, or subtle and luminous colors, their atmosphere of tragedy, their flow of life and vitality, their hint of the irrepressible, the immediate, the unrefined, and the elementary, these paintings transcribe the whole totality of our being and of the longed-for object of our quest.

To renounce knowledge, culture, and will. To renounce resistance and self-affirmation. To experience some fifty years of crushing poverty and the drama of absolute solitude. To suffer humiliation. To meet during that interminable period with nothing but indifference, incomprehension, and even sarcasm . . .

I love this good, simple, lucid, spare, transparent, hypersensitive, serene and savage man, with his solitude, his love of silence, his tragedy, and his vivacity, this man who has had the well-nigh superhuman courage to endure the worst and never deviate from his path.

This man who lives and has lived a life so self-effacing that, in the course of his whole, long existence, there have been scarcely more than a handful of people who have ever really paid any attention to him or suspected what possessed him.

This man in whom I have so often felt the pulse of the most alive. Who showed at each of our meetings that he was always thinking most profoundly.

This painter, this inspired man. Consumed by his thirst for the fundamental.

November, 1978

What strikes you on meeting Bram van Velde is his distinction, his surprising timidity, his gentleness, his simplicity, his interminable silences, and, when he breaks them, the density of what he says.

In reality, this man is a solitary person, someone permanently turned inward, a seeker of the absolute.

"Painting is touching the truth. It's forcing the vision that I need to rise up. It's looking for the face that has no face."

That's why he spends his days alone, meditating, waiting for the need to paint to become irrepressible and push him toward the canvas. But, most of the time, the energy needed to access this place of greatest intensity is lacking. So he must arm himself with patience, endure the emptiness of the hours, and, above all, not try to provoke this same rising up that he desires so passionately. This is the experience of undesire, non-knowledge, and inability.

"The most difficult thing is to do nothing. You have to be deprived of all means. You have to let go. Trust in a deep oblivion."

When he lived in Carouge, Bram had no studio. He worked in a garage, and because it had no heat, he could only paint during the summer months. He completed two, maybe three big gouaches and one or two inks for a book or a catalogue. And this, along with a few lithographs, made up his entire year's production.

By refusing to have a studio, Bram made sure that he lived in accordance with his destitute past, with the material and spiritual combat that had always underlain his path through life, his existence.

In Paris, he works in the room where he lives. A room on the third floor, long and narrow, lit by two windows facing the inside courtyard of a building.

Except for a few clothes, Beckett's books, and a few catalogues dedicated to him, Bram van Velde owns nothing.

Next to the bed, standing on a chair, a wooden panel on which a white sheet of paper is tacked. Next to it, on a small table, four or five paintbrushes, two plates plastered with dried and mixed paint, a few tubes of paint, a small bottle of India ink, and a glass three-quarters full of cloudy water. This is everything that Bram uses to create his works, which capture something of the eternal.

When I meet Bram, zero conversation. After a preliminary "How are you?" we sit down in silence. And then, I rediscover Bram and his concentration, his steadfast preoccupation with the essential, the power of his being, his acuity of thought, his radiance.

This Sunday is a sluggish winter day. Black sky, heavy rain. Profound silence. Bram hasn't opened his mouth for more than twenty-four hours. And, at noon, lacking the energy to go down to the restaurant, he nibbled at a few cookies. He is tense, somber, extremely sorrowful.

From time to time, he blurts out a sentence. And perhaps to excuse himself for not being able to converse with me better:

"Painting has amputated my words. When I speak, I am always doing so illegally."

After a moment, with an unfocused gaze:

"I am dead in the mouth."

A silence that stretches. Then, as if gripped by a sudden revelation, as though he is the first to have thought it, he murmurs in a devastated voice:

"We are all born dead."

Sorry to break into his meditation, I occasionally risk asking a question. But I never know if it reaches him, since a long silence inevitably follows it. Then his response gushes out, heavy with life experience, with suffering; once spoken, it goes on resounding inside you:

"This isn't painting for pleasure. It's painting to live."

There follows a moment of great intensity when he tries to explain the necessity that he feels to want nothing, to force nothing.

"That's where everything is played out."

You have to deny all support, all barriers, all obstacles—culture, logic, good taste, savoir faire, the weight of everything that's already been achieved—and let yourself be swallowed up.

When he paints, he exists only in his movement, and the color that, he confides to me, *comes out of him*. The painting finished, he no longer knows where he is.

"If you want the work to have something living, there has to be a death."

The artist has to allow himself to be erased, to disappear; this is the only state in which what he wants to draw out of himself has a chance of being transfused into what his hands are creating.

He goes on to speak to me, fiercely, of the freedom which he feels he must attain. A total, absolute freedom. Because the smallest attachment, constraint, restriction, the least desire, frightens life away, kills it before it has a chance to be.

And he adds, with a seriousness so grave that you can feel the meaning of every word:

"One can live without freedom. Without the unknown.

"It is terribly difficult to really 'be.'"

August-September, 1979—Grimaud

We arrived this morning. We'll stay three weeks to keep Bram company.

A strong smell of lavender. A bit of wind. Far away, the chains of hills are veiled by a haze of heat.

I'm sitting next to Bram beneath a cork oak, at the corner of the terrace.

"I have only one desire," he explains to me, "to see the unknown that's in me. To see is to live. To live is to see. Painting lets one see what is seen."

He talks again about fear. Fear of all the horrors that make up life. He says he is constantly afraid.

"We are so fragile. So powerless. Painting is a response."

He is painting two big gouaches, but he'll show them to me later. He wants to be able to see them with a fresh eye, and he needs to let a few days pass.

"Painting allows me to achieve non-work. A higher state. I prefer doing nothing. So many things arise out of silence and immobility.

"Painting is born of the greatest extremes. You have to let yourself be carried. Let yourself go through it. But it is rare that one is capable of total abandon."

That evening, after dinner, in the fading light, we speak about the truth, Kafka, Beckett . . .

With regard to the latter:

"His work has no waste. To attain such a density . . ."

A long silence.

I tell him he is less a painter than an adventurer. An adventurer of the internal life. A mystic (and I clarify that I use the word outside of all reference to any kind of transcendence whatsoever). A being whose existence is subject to a passionate and persistent pursuit of life.

He smiles. After a long silence:

"When not pursuing, it's inevitable that one loses oneself in emptiness."

His immense solitude. But how could he be otherwise? It is inevitable that someone who never stops developing should one day find himself distanced from the rest of his kind.

As is so often the case, I think he is sorrowful, but neither sad nor demoralized.

I've been here for three days, but he still doesn't want us to go look at the two gouaches he just finished.

After dinner, we meet in the living room. I leaf through a catalogue of contemporary American painting, and we talk about a few of these painters. Then he concludes:

"Most artists are concerned with perfecting their own little specialty—those who think about the whole are rare.

"A good number of painters and writers don't know how to separate themselves from culture, from tradition. Often, they create from knowledge."

He returns to the observation that there is no word, no language to express what a being experiences at its deepest levels.

"A man who stays in contact with his interior can't help but be devoured by fear. What he goes through in his private life doesn't count for anything in the so-called real world."

He explains that he has always felt like an exile.

"The more intensely one's internal reality is lived, the less one can and does know how to express it."

What's always struck me about him is, on the one hand, his ability to formulate such a fragile reality, such a dazzling instant of his interior process in just a few words, and, on the other, his incapacity to explain or develop what he's just proposed. A flash of lightning goes through him, collects into one brief sentence, and then, nothing, silence. Once again, I find myself confirming the distinction that I've made between deep thoughts and thoughts arising from the intellect.

At the end of the afternoon, we were sitting at the other end of the terrace, near the laurels. The weather was extremely mild and we savored those moments of relative freshness and profound silence. But the caretaker's son—eight years old—soon appeared on his little motorbike, and for three-quarters of an hour kept passing back and forth in front of us, wanting to be admired. We said goodbye to the silence and charm of that afternoon, because neither Bram nor I had the heart to end his so-obvious pleasure.

Bram reminds me of the story that he heard from Beckett, about the writer and the concierge's radio. After laughing, he quotes the inscription on Paul Valéry's tomb—or rather, the inscription Valéry had wanted:

Here lies Paul Valéry
Killed by others.

Here, he now has a small studio at his disposal. He leaves the door open. The panels supporting the two gouaches are just lying on the floor. In our absence, the two big dogs that keep us company could have knocked them over, or even urinated on them. But Bram is indifferent. Dozens of fat, noisy flies have found refuge in this place. Sheets of paper are strewn on the floor.

The first gouache (a bit more than two meters by approximately one and a third meters): blacks, reds, and whites outline sweeping forms in the course of their evolution. Will they stabilize, or, on the contrary, be torn apart by the tensions that run through them? One cannot know.

The second gouache (same format): blacks, purples, and large preserved white spaces. This is the stronger of the two, the more intense. Both are wild, disheveled, giving the impression of something raw, unfinished. It takes some time to really see them, really perceive them. Partitions define areas that seem poorly articulated, although one feels an organic interdependence between them.

I admire that he can forget his acquired skills to this extent, to paint almost like a beginner. But a beginner who has had sixty years of practice, who can spontaneously access the unpremeditated, who possesses the art of transparency, refinement, the art of the unfinished that leaves the work open to a possible future.

Two of our friends came to visit, and the presence of these two people who don't know his painting pushes him to chime out a few comments:

"When it comes down to it, everything always goes back to this question: What is life?

"By painting, I liberate myself from fear.

"This act of liberation is also the pursuit of liberty.

"To liberate myself from the intolerable . . .

"It's an act of life. A primitive act.

"Painting speaks the language of silence.

"I don't look to make a painting. The painting itself is much less important than what it allows me to attain.

"It's the power, the magic of painting that's kept me on my feet."

Contemplating the canvases, there is an intense sensation of life. Certainly these paintings are tragic. And yet joy circulates here, more and more present. You feel you can see the great forces that move in us represented here, the forces that push us, tear us apart, and I think again that all great art is anonymous, because it brings the universal part of us, our common roots, to life.

Our friends stay, and after dinner, in the living room, where we pass the evening, we look at the paintings that Bram did in Worpswede, fifty-six years ago. He tells us that he remembers painting each one of his works, as well as the time and place where it was painted.

"Memory is a curious thing. It's because painting is tied to life. Everything else is blotted out, but these instants of life remain.

"I have to feel pushed toward the canvas. If there isn't this impetus, I can't do it. I have to wait."

He tells us what admiration he has for Franz Hals and Rembrandt. Talks to us about them as only a painter can.

We mention Fromentin, Baudelaire . . . I remind him what he told me about the latter: ". . . he knew how to not embellish."

"Yes," he acquiesces, "he didn't let himself be seduced by beauty. For him, passion tore apart and supplanted beauty."

He speaks to us about Nicolas de Staël, who came to find him and brought him to his studio. He was determined to get Bram's opinion about what he had painted. But there were so many canvases in his studio that Bram couldn't see anything and didn't know what to say. He explains that he can only look at three or four paintings at a time, never more.

Our visit ends. Bram remained beneath his tree for entire days, looking off into the distance at the swell of the hills. Health problems prevented him from going back to work and I ask him if he is disappointed.

"No, no. Two big gouaches, that's a good year."

Notes
Adriaan van der Weel and Ruud Hisgen

Annotations for both *Conversations with Samuel Beckett* and *Conversations with Bram van Velde* have been kept deliberately light. Texts and people especially relevant to Van Velde and Beckett have been identified, but artists who can be readily found in standard reference works have been omitted. To avoid tiring the reader with endless references in the footnotes, the main factual and biographical sources are credited here:

Deirdre Bair, *Samuel Beckett: A Biography,* New York & London, 1978.

Hans Janssen, "Een schildersleven," in *Bram van Velde 1895–1981,* The Hague, 1989, pp. 9–37.

Jacques Putman, *Bram van Velde,* Paris, 1975.

Erik Slagter, *Bram van Velde: Een hommage,* exhibition catalogue, Leiden, Zoeterwoude, Schiedam en Deurne, 1994.

1. The French literary critic who was one of the first to recognize Beckett's stature.

2. Henri Hayden was a painter friend Beckett first met during his stay in Roussillon in 1942.

3. Jérôme Lindon, one of the founders of the publishing house that published all of Beckett's work in French, and who was to become a good friend of Beckett's.

4. The actress was renowned for her performances of Beckett's work. The play is *Not I.*

5. The Irish friend was actually his cousin Maurice Sinclair.

6. Jacques Putnam, *Bram van Velde*, Paris, 1975.

7. Bernard of Clairvaux, twelfth-century Cistercian abbot; it's possible that the "grudge" Beckett bears him is due to Clairvaux's biography of St. Malachy, which popularized the notion that Ireland was a land of barbarians. [Editor's Note]

8. See note 38 to *Conversations with Bram van Velde.*

9. The *Mirlitonnades* have not been translated.

1. Putman is also the author of the authoritative monograph *Bram van Velde*, Paris, 1975; trans. New York, 1975. From the 1960s onward Van Velde increasingly makes use of Putman's two houses: in Paris and Grimaud. In 1981 he was buried in Putman's burial plot in Aries.

2. In 1959.

3. Born Lisse (Netherlands), 1898; died Cachan (France), 1977.

4. Born The Hague, 1903; died Amsterdam, 1985. She was a writer in her own right (publishing at first under the pseudonym of Tonny Clerx), but also translated a substantial number of Beckett's works, and helped Beckett find publishers.

5. Paris, 1946.

6. Galerie Knoedler, New York; Walker Art Center, Minneapolis; San Francisco Museum of Art; Colorado Springs Fine Art Center, 1964–1965.

7. By Louis-Ferdinand Céline.

8. The Museo d'Arte Moderna.

9. *Malone Dies*, Penguin, 1962, pp. 20–21. Though they are rarely very literal translations, all English versions of the French quotations from Beckett's writings presented in this volume are Beckett's own, unless otherwise indicated.

10. Madeleine Spierer, with whom he shared a home in Geneva from 1962 to 1977.

11. First published in *Les Cahiers dart nos* 20–21 (1945–46), pp. 349–56; repr. in *Disjecta: Miscellaneous Writings and a Dramatic*

Fragment, ed. Ruby Cohn, London, 1983, pp. 127 and 130; trans. Janey Tucker.

12. The informal form of the French second-person pronoun.

13. From "La peinture des Van Velde ou le monde et le pantalon," in *Disjecta*, p. 127; trans. Janey Tucker.

14. Interview by Gabriel d'Aubarède, *Les nouvelles littéraires*, 1746 (16 February 1961), pp. 1 and 7, on p. 7.

15. *L'unique*, Maeght, Paris, 1973.

16. *La folie du jour*, Montpellier, 1973.

17. Paris, 1972; English translation: *Louvre Dialogues*, New York, 1972.

18. "Bram van Velde," the third of the "Three Dialogues with Georges Duthuit," *transition* no 5 (1949); repr. in *Proust*, pp. 95–126; quotation on p. 119.

19. See Note 1 to *Conversations with Samuel Beckett*.

20. "Hommage à Jack B. Yeats," April 1954; repr. in *Disjecta*, with Beckett's English translation, pp. 148–49.

21. Georges Duthuit was the editor of the postwar resurrection of Eugene Jolas's *transition*.

22. "Denn die Herrlichkeit ist nur ein Augenblick, und wir haben nie etwas Längeres gesehen als das Elend," from *Die Aufzeichnungen des Malte Laurids Brigge, Sämtliche Werke*, 6 vols, ed. Ernst Zinn, Wiesbaden, Frankfurt, 1955–66, vol. 6, pp. 905–6.

23. No 11 in Jacques Putman's *Bram van Velde*.

24. Written in English; published London, 1931; repr. in *Proust*; quotation on p. 64.

25. Luchino Visconti's *Death in Venice* (1970).

26. They were published in facsimile as *Le carnet de Bayonne*, Paris, 1974.

27. It has not been possible to trace publication details for this interview.

28. Jacques Demougin, "Les plongés de Bram van Velde," *Les nouvelles littéraires*, 21 November 1968, p. 11. The retrospective at the Musée National d'Art Moderne was in the Winter of 1970/71. The occasion may have been an exhibition in Galerie Knoedler, Paris.

29. Actually, from "Peintres de l'empêchement," published in *Derrière le miroir*, Paris, 1948; repr. in *Disjecta*; this quotation on pp. 136–37. The English given here is Beckett's own translation, published in the exhibition catalogue for Van Velde's first exhibition in New York (Samuel Kootz Gallery, March 1948).

30. Bruno Roy is the publisher of Editions Fata Morgana. This and the following conversations were published in the augmented edition of *Rencontres avec Bram van Velde* in 1978.

31. Entitled *Bram van Velde*, 1963.

32. Robert Wilson; *Deafman Glance* was first staged in the U.S. in 1970.

33. Carlos Castaneda, *The Teachings of Don Juan: A Yaqui Way of Knowledge*, 1969.

34. "On Murder Considered as One of the Fine Arts," first paper, in *The Collected Writings of Thomas de Quincey*, 14 vols, Edinburgh, 1889–1890, vol. 13, *Tales and Prose Phantasies*, on pp. 24–27.

35. Alfred Kollmar (1886–1937) was a major early influence on Van Velde.

36. Marthe Arnaud was the pseudonym of Marthe Kuntz, with whom Van Velde had a relationship after the death of his first wife, Lilly Klöker.

37. Putman.

38. Madeleine Spierer turned Van Velde out of her house in Geneva, and burnt a number of his works in the garden.

39. "Wer das Tiefste gedacht, liebt das Lebendigste," from "Sokrates und Alcibiades," *Sämtliche Werken*, Stuttgart 1943–1977, vol. I, 1, *Gedichte bis 1800*, p. 260.

40. "[. . .] du [. . .] suchst das Größte und das Schönste nur," from *Hyperion*, vol. i, part 2, *Sämtliche Werken*, vol. III, *Hyperion*, p. 89.

Charles Juliet was born in 1934 in Jujurieux, France and lives today in Lyon. He attended military school until age twenty, when he entered the École de Sante Militaire in Lyon. Three years later, he gave up his studies and began writing, working in solitude for more than a decade before his first book was published.

SELECTED DALKEY ARCHIVE PAPERBACKS

FOR A FULL LIST OF PUBLICATIONS, VISIT:
www.dalkeyarchive.com